the

weaver's studio

rep weave

and beyond

the
weaver's studio

rep
weave
and beyond

Joanne Tallarovic

INTERWEAVE PRESS
www.interweave.com

Editor: Marilyn Murphy
Technical Editor: Judie Eatough
Copy Editor: Betsy Strauch
Illustrations: Judie Eatough
Photography: Joe Coca
Process Photography: Tom Alexander
Photo Styling: Ann Swanson
Cover and Page Design: Karen Schober
Production: Dean Howes
Proofreader and Indexer: Nancy Arndt

Interweave Press, Inc.
201 East Fourth Street
Loveland, Colorado 80537 USA
www.interweave.com

Printed and bound in Singapore

Library of Congress Cataloging-in-Publication Data

Tallarovic, Joanne, 1943-
 Rep weave and beyond / Joanne Tallarovic.
    p. cm.
 Includes bibliographical references.
 ISBN 1-931499-45-4
 1. Hand weaving. I. Title.
 TX848.T253 2004
 746.1'4--dc22

                    2004001076

10 9 8 7 6 5 4 3 2 1

Dedication

This book is dedicated in loving memory to Denise Kavanagh, my good friend, colleague, and fellow traveler to Scandinavia. Denise continually encouraged me to put everything I know about rep weave into print for weaving students and American handweavers. I promised that I would. I had just begun when she passed away in December 2002.

Acknowledgments

I am grateful to the following people, who helped me to carry through my dream: Bob Tallarovic, for his encouragement, patience, reading, rereading, and waiting for late dinners; Matthew and Sara, who as children rode the treadles of my Cranbrook loom and learned to love and appreciate textiles from both sides; my mother, Belle, who put fabrics in my hands at a young age and taught me to love textiles; Judie Eatough, student, friend, and mentor, who said, "When you're ready to do the book, call me." Judie taught me about computers, working tricks I never dreamed possible, and created all the drafts in the book; June Gilliam and staff at Gilliam's Center for Creative Design and the Es Posible Gallery, in Scottsdale, Arizona, for their steadfast loyalty and promotion of my work; Carolyn and Frank Batchelor, Ann and Arnold Johnson, Sue and Bill Martin, Jenny Blue and Rick Moore, Caryl and Dick Marcusen, and Susanna Brock, who loaned artwork from their private collections; the friends, supporters, and students who encouraged me; and the many people at Interweave Press who made this book a reality, especially Marilyn Murphy for her sensitive and comprehensive editing in putting this book into a cohesive form for weavers of all levels—thanks for everything.

contents

Introduction

For the past twenty years, I've explored Swedish ripsmatta, or rep weave, and developed new ways of using it. The term "ripsmatta" is a combination of the Swedish words rips ("rep") and matta ("mat"). American handweavers know it as a warp-faced rug technique that produces a ridged fabric.

My dedication to this kind of weaving dates back to 1962–1967, when I was a student at the Cleveland Institute of Art. There I was exposed to Scandinavian weaving and a traditional approach to weaving and design. The solid and lasting weaving ethic instilled in me has had a profound effect on my weaving career. During those years, I had the good fortune to weave on a Scandinavian-style countermarch loom, unaware that much later I would get hooked on rep weave and the countermarch loom would be an advantage. I purchased my first loom in 1966, a 6-shaft, 8-treadle countermarch Cranbrook. Until 2000, when I bought an 8-shaft loom, I was content to design and weave on fewer shafts. On occasion, when a fabric design required more shafts, I worked around my loom's limitations by threading more blocks on shafts already in use and using a pick-up stick to either pick up or push down the threads I didn't need in each shed. Forced to improvise to create the fabric I wanted, I made the loom work in ways that I needed at the moment. I am convinced that I learned more about rep weave because of that limitation than if I'd woven on more shafts from the beginning.

In the 1980s, when I began weaving rep, little on the technique had been published in English. When, in 1986 and 1987, two Swedish books were published in English, numerous other American handweavers and I were eager to try the patterns. We were not attuned to threading thousands of fine cotton warp threads (usually 90-plus ends per inch with two threads in each heddle), nor were our looms already equipped with enough heddles to do so. At the time, we were daunted by having to thread more than 20 ends per inch, and the standard Swedish weft materials of thick string or cotton roving weren't very exciting. And for the weavers who were working on jack or counterbalance looms, they had a difficult time opening a shed with such dense warp. The Swedish weave was simply too tedious and cumbersome for us.

But because I really liked the look of rep weave, I began searching for a way to adapt and modify this technique to make it more feasible. If I could find a warp thread in a wide color range that was large enough to sley single in the heddle instead of double, if I could use fewer heddles, and if I could sett the warp so that it mimicked the look of rep, I would be able to emulate the look and feel of Swedish rep without the rigor of the traditional approach.

I had been weaving 2-block log cabin placemats and rag rugs with Maysville 8/4 cotton carpet warp. This sturdy thread was readily available and seemed a logical warp choice. Instead of setting warps at the traditional 90 ends per inch, I sett them at different densities and changed setts with each warp I put on the loom. Multiple colors in the warp resulted in a more complex color interaction of warp and weft, and vice versa. I wove hundreds of placemats, runners, and rugs, each time setting the warp differently to investigate just what was happening with each change. At the same time, I began using a wide range of printed fabric wefts in place of the traditional thick cotton string. This helped me to identify how different fibers behaved and to discover that they interacted with the warp in surprising and unexpected ways. More important, I learned that using more shafts resulted in more color interplay in the weave, producing fabrics whose appearance and performance differed greatly from those of traditional rep.

It was by happenstance that I discovered that the methods that worked for my rugs and runners also could be used to produce lighter fabrics. By trying very fine threads to get a lightweight, supple fabric, by opening up the setts to get garment-weight cloth, by using fabric strips as weft to achieve complex color patterning, I've been able to make towels, clothing, gift cards, wall hangings, and more. Over the years, I have pushed rep weave well beyond its traditional use as a rug technique. What I hope to do in this book is to lead you through my thought processes along with the step-by-step weaving procedures that have worked for me.

This book is meant to be a resource for weavers—a workbook to instruct and serve as inspiration. I hope that it will introduce you to a new way of finding, seeing, and using color and techniques in your weaving. I will continue to explore and hope this book encourages you to do the same.

Theory

he rep technique has been known in various cultures since early times. Excavations in Peru and Egypt have unearthed fragments dating back to the fourth century. Asians for centuries have used rep-weave remnants as camel girths. And today in Central Asia, long, narrow, colorful rep-woven bands are used to bind together sections of framework for yurts covered with felted wool.

Swedish Rep Vs New Rep

Both traditional Swedish rep and what I'm calling "new rep" are warp-faced block weaves. Each block has two faces or colors that alternate in the warp. Weavers of Swedish rep refer to these faces as "dark" and "light"; I call them "pattern" and "background." Either way, one of the colors is raised for a thick weft and the other for a thin weft so that the first color shows on the surface while the second shows on the back (or vice versa). The traditional Swedish technique differs from what I do—in warp type and size, denting, setts, choice of weft materials, and loom modifications—but it provides a good foundation for understanding where I've taken it.

Swedish Rep

What I know of Swedish rep (ripsmatta in Swedish) comes from three study trips to Scandinavia and from my reading. The kind of rugs I'm familiar with are known as far back as the mid-1800s. Although it's hard to date these early rugs because household records weren't kept, it is known that the first cotton mills in Sweden were founded about this time; textile factories still remain in the area around Borås. The industry also developed about forty miles to the west around Göteborg, a port where cheap American cotton was unloaded. Since cotton was strong and easy to spin, dye, and wash, it quickly replaced linen and hemp as warp in the rugs. By the mid-twentieth century, two-ply cotton warp was in production and was the most common warp of choice for Swedish rug weavers. Patterns, influenced by other weaving techniques from different regions of the country, included stripes, overshot derivatives, and monk's belt. Traditional rugs often contained thousands of warp threads, and some are said to have lasted more than 100 years.

Written drafts and records dating from the mid-1850s to the present indicate that traditional Swedish rep weave has been woven the same way with little variation. It's usually woven as a two-color reversible stripe or check with a very closely sett warp covering the weft completely except at the edges. The warps, generally of two highly contrasting colors, continue to be made of 16/2 cotton threaded two threads in the heddle, four threads in the dent, 90–100 ends per inch. *Rep Weaves* by Laila Lundell, former headmistress of Handarbettes Vennar in Stockholm, presents this traditional approach using 16/2 cotton for warp with hundreds, even thousands of ends in the rug. *Rep* by Catharina Carlstedt and Ylva Kongbäck takes a more modern view, varying some of the warps by using 16/2 linen, 8/8 cotton roving yarn, or 28/2 worsted yarn. But as in *Rep*'s woven projects, many use fine warps of 16/2 cotton warp sett at 90 ends (45 pairs) per inch, with two threads in the heddle and four per dent in a 22.5-dent reed.

The wefts in traditional Swedish ripsmatta are alternately thick and thin. The thick weft consists of white 3/5 cotton string, used singly or bundled three to four strands together, or 2/2 cotton, used singly or bundled six strands together. Thin wefts may be

From the collection of the Nordic Heritage Museum, Seattle, Washington, 91.185.1; cotton, dark pink and white, 22³/₄ × 254³/₄.

16/2, single or doubled. Thick wefts serve as filler and cause the warp to produce the color pattern and textural rib on the surface. The weft, which is visible only at the selvedge anyway, can be made even less noticeable by making it the same color as the edge stripe in the warp, or a coordinating color.

Jack, countermarch, and counterbalance looms are all available in Sweden, but the loom of choice for rep is traditionally the counterbalance, modified as described below to accommodate the dense warp. The method used in threading, tie-up, and treadling of a given type of loom differs depending on its shedding mechanism. Most 2-block patterns are threaded on four shafts even though only two treadles are required. The mere density of the warp demands that the warp be threaded onto twice as many shafts as there are blocks to obtain an adequate shed. Weaves with two blocks are threaded on opposites, for example, Block A on shafts 1 and 4 and Block B on 2 and 3.

When using more design blocks necessitates threading onto more shafts to obtain a better shed, the simple counterbalance pulley and rocker arms—nickepinne—are replaced with a dräll pulley system. A dräll is a teardrop-shaped fixture containing nine small wheels, one at the bottom and four on either side running upward in parallel. Drälls are used in pairs hung from a crossbar and spaced at the midpoint of each half of the warp. A cord traveling horizontally over parallel wheels and attached to the heddle bars moves the shafts up or down in opposite pairs. As one shaft of the pair rises, the other one falls. A greater space exists between the center pair of shafts 2 and 3, which would normally be attached to the lower wheel cord, thus allowing the warp to move more freely. Eight shafts and ten treadles are normally used for 4-block patterns. The four blocks are threaded on shafts 1–8, 2–7, 3–6, and 4–5. Treadles are generally tied in adjacent pairs with opposite tie-up combinations. In Swedish publications, a black square in the tie-up draft indicates a sinking shaft, and an open square indicates a rising shaft. On a countermarch loom, the shaft indicated in the tie-up by a black square is tied to the short or upper lamm (which sinks the shaft), and the shaft indicated in the tie-up by an open square is tied to the long or lower lamm (which raises the shaft).

In the threading draft, a black square represents the pattern threads, and a slash represents the background threads.

New Rep

When I began to weave rep, I became focused on finding a thicker thread that would allow me to sett the warp less densely than the traditional Swedish sett but achieve a similar look. I found that I could use 8/4 cotton carpet warp for rugs, tableware, and decorative hangings, using setts of 16–30 ends per inch threaded single in the heddle, double in the dent, or 16–20 pairs (32–40 ends per inch) double in the heddle, four ends per dent. I use 8- to 15-dent reeds double-sleyed, 8- and 10-dent reeds quadruple-sleyed. All three types of looms—jack, countermarch, and counterbalance—are capable of sufficient shedding with these setts without altering the shedding mechanism. I can thread a given number of blocks on the same number of shafts, making more design blocks possible, and I thread the blocks on pairs of adjacent shafts, one next to

the other, inverting the threading order to create additional blocks.

Because the setts are more open, the weft shows through to varying degrees, producing a livelier, more dynamic surface. For my thick wefts, I often use new fabric, even printed calico (old or recycled clothing or bed linens may also be used), cutting two 1-inch-wide strips of printed fabric and winding them together on a shuttle. For the thin weft, I use a shot of 8/4 cotton carpet warp. The fabric gives the finished weaving a nice thickness and hand.

Rather than the traditional two-color warp, I blend many colors in the pattern and/or background blocks, requiring many color changes and splicing of threads during warping. To describe these new methods, I've coined some new terms, such as constants, outline threads, and phantom blocks, which I explain in Design with Blocks for Rep (page 50).

Although the Swedish approach needs two shafts per block because the warp is so dense, my more open sett lets me thread many blocks in a pattern on the same number of shafts without causing shedding difficulties. Therefore, a 4-block pattern threaded on four shafts at the maximum single sett of 30 ends per inch does not require an 8-shaft threading to give an adequate shed for weaving.

In my tie-up and treadling drafts, I indicate the rising sheds with numbers. Adjacent treadles are tied in pairs; a solid square represents the thick (fabric) weft, and a slashed square represents the thin weft.

During weaving, each pick of thick weft ordinarily is tied down with a pick of thin weft in the opposite shed before moving to the next pattern shed. If the tie-down shed happens to be the next pattern shed, however, the tie-down is omitted and replaced by the thick weft, which is then followed by a tie-down pick. In the new rep, I don't carry the thick and thin wefts together in the same shed as the thin pick tends to crawl up and lie on top of the thick weft. Although not immediately apparent, the thin weft eventually moves, becomes visible, and looks like a mistake.

If you've woven rep in the traditional Swedish manner, the new rep may seem peculiar at first, but do give it a try. You might get hooked just like I did. And if you've never woven rep before, follow my approach and have fun.

Warping

've detailed in this section my tried-and-true warping procedure—the one I've used for the past forty years. I wind my warps on a large, vertical warping mill as I usually make 20-yard warps. However, if you're warping shorter lengths, a small warping mill or a board will accomplish the same thing.

I beam the warp from back to front because, for me, it's quicker, the cross is never cut (see Warping the Loom, page 25), and there is no need to untangle or "comb" the warp as you wind. There is also less warp abrasion when you beam first, then thread, than when you pull an entire warp through the reed and heddles. But that's only a preference and I do consider them advantages; you may be more comfortable warping from front to back. No matter which method you choose, take your time and be patient as you prepare your warp—it's one of the keys to a happy and successful weaving.

Warp Preparation

Preparing to weave rep differs from preparing to weave other structures, particularly in calculating how long to make your warp. Although shrinkage occurs in all weaving, rep weave that uses a thick fabric weft consumes an astonishing 34% of warp length in the combined take-up during weaving and shrinkage once the weaving is off the loom. This great loss is due to a combination of tight tension used to weave rep and the use of fabric as weft. (On the other hand, weaving clothing-weight yardage in rep weave consumes about 10% warp length in take-up and shrinkage—similar to that occurring in other weave structures.) My own costly mistakes in estimating materials have reinforced the importance of careful calculation and record keeping. Accuracy during the planning stages is the first step toward eliminating potential problems.

Calculating Materials

Record all of the following details when planning your project.

PROJECT NOTES

Warp List manufacturer, size, fiber, and yardage per pound, tube, or skein, and color number.

Weft List each weft. For each, list manufacturer, size, fiber, yardage, color, and amount needed. Note the type of shuttle used for each weft—rug, rag, boat, etc.

Warp Sett Ends per inch, the number of threads per heddle and dent.

Reed The number of dents per inch.

Width in Reed The width the warp will spread in the reed.

Finished Width The estimated width after weaving. The width of the warp in the reed usually remains the same. The width of the piece itself may be slightly wider because the fabric weft extends a bit beyond the warp selvedge.

Total Ends Multiply the width in reed times the number of ends per inch.

Cloth Length The *finished, woven* length of a piece—the length off the loom including shrinkage but not hems or fringes.

Raw Length The actual length that must be woven to compensate for 17% shrinkage (see Shrinkage, below). To calculate this length, divide the cloth length by 0.83.

Take-Up The length of warp taken up due to the thickness of the fabric weft and weaving under very tight tension. Seventeen percent of the woven length is lost to take-up during weaving.

Shrinkage The relaxation of the warp *after* the weaving is off the loom—relaxed, ironed, steamed, starched, massaged, handled, etc. Seventeen percent of the woven length is lost to shrinkage.

Tie-On The length needed to tie the warp to the front and back tie-rods. This allowance can be untied and used for fringe and should be noted as such.

Hems Plan about 1³/₄" woven with 8/4 carpet warp, about twenty picks, for a twice-folded (three-layered) hem. This allowance is not needed if the tie-on becomes fringe.

Loom Waste The length of warp between the fell line and back tie-rod that cannot be woven due to lack of shed. It is proportionate to the number of shafts on the loom. Generally, allow 4" per shaft as loom waste. This length can be used for a fringe.

Total Warp Length The total length of a warp including cloth length, take-up, shrinkage, tie-on, hems or fringe, and loom waste designated in inches and also rounded to the nearest quarter-yard.

Warp Color Order The order in which the warp threads are wound on the warping board or mill.

Threading The order in which the heddles are threaded.

Tie-Up The combination of shafts that raise together.

Treadling Draft The order in which the shafts are raised.

A good way to ensure that all aspects of warp length have been addressed is to draw a layout of the project in your weaving notes. Label the different parts along with measurements.

Winding the Warp

Assemble the warp plan, yarns, scissors, tape measure, notebook, and pencil (Figure 1).

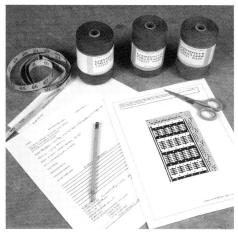

FIGURE 1

Make a measuring string the length of your warp plus about 10"; tie a loop at the end of the string. Place the loop on the last peg closest to where the cross (the figure eight that keeps the warp ends in order) will be made on the warping board or mill (Figure 2). Use the string to

FIGURE 2

trace the path of the warp from the beginning to the opposite end of the board or mill. Tie the end of the string to the peg that comes closest to the required length (Figure 3).

FIGURE 3

Loading the Spool Rack

The spool rack is used not to beam sectionally but to hold all the warp spools, in color order based on the warp color order chart, in position so that you can wind the warp in a straight line to the warping board or mill. Load a spool rack in the order that warp colors will be used, orienting the spools so that the thread ends all pull from the bottom (Figure 1). This helps keep threads from plying together as the spools unwind. If you are winding from a stand, all spools should unwind in the same clockwise or counterclockwise direction. Follow the warp order plan in the project notes for your project.

FIGURE 1

Wind by placing a finger between threads and always place a new thread above the previous one on the mill or board. Make sure the threads stay in the correct warp order from spool to mill (Figure 2). Some projects suggest winding the warp in two sections, half at a time. This eliminates the build up of warp on the board or mill.

FIGURE 2

Splicing the Warp

When it's time to change a warp color—which I often do—you will need to splice in a new warp end. To do this, cut off the thread to be deleted near the top or bottom peg of the warping board or mill (Figure 1). To avoid tangles, wind up the end of the cut-off thread back onto the spool before proceeding. Take off the old color spool first and replace it with the new color. Pull out the end of the new color, and tie the ends of the old and new colors with an overhand knot (Figure 2); continue to wind with the new color.

FIGURE 1

FIGURE 2

Counting Warp Ends

You can decide how often to count, but I count several times during the warping process to assure accuracy as I wind. Counting the warp ends takes place at the cross. With both hands held palms up, insert your index fingers into each opening at the cross, then curl the end of these fingers up slightly (Figure 1).

Exert a slight pressure on the warp and straighten the right finger to allow a warp (or warps) to slide off it (Figure 2). Straighten the left finger, counting as the threads slip off (Figure 3). Continue to alternate and count, placing a pre-cut string around every twenty to forty threads to help you keep track of the total number of ends (Figure 4).

FIGURE 1

FIGURE 3

FIGURE 2

FIGURE 4

Tying the Cross

There are several ways of tying the cross; I like to use a single string. Cut a strong string about 24" long and lay the center of the string over the top of the warp on one side of the cross (Figure 1). Insert one of the cut ends directly through the opening created by the cross, then bring the other cut end through in the opposite direction (Figures 2 and 3). Cross the cut ends underneath and bring each one upward, in opposite directions, through the other half of the cross (Figures 4 and 5). After isolating the four sections of the cross with the string, tie the ends in an overhand knot on top of the

FIGURE 1

FIGURE 2

FIGURE 4

FIGURE 3

FIGURE 5

FIGURE 6

warp. This will be the only knot in the warp chain; all others will be bow ties that release quickly and easily during beaming (Figure 6). Compress the warp and tie every 1-yard on the mill or board using a cinch and bow tie (Figures 7 and 8).

Chaining

Begin the warp chain at the end opposite the cross. Hold the warp while removing the peg, or lifting the warp off the peg from the board or mill, taking care not to let the warp fall off the board or mill (Figures 1 and 2). Hold the

FIGURE 7

FIGURE 1

FIGURE 8

FIGURE 2

loop with your left hand and keep a slight tension on the warp as you work (Figure 3). Insert your right hand through the loop and grasp the warp, pulling it through the loop. Change hands so your left hand is holding the warp and continue to chain until 1 yard of warp remains. Do not pull the cross end through the loop, but tie the remaining warp to the chain using a cinch and bow tie. Record the warp weight and date wound in your notebook for future reference (Figures 4–7).

FIGURE 3

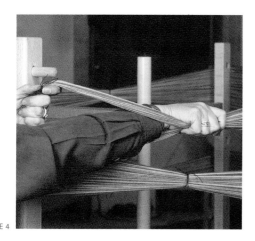

FIGURE 4

FIGURE 5

FIGURE 6

FIGURE 7

Warping the Loom

Warping the loom is an exacting task, but doing it carefully and correctly will reward you with smoother weaving and better results. The following instructions are based on the Scandinavian method of warping *from back to front*. Accurate, quick and trouble-free, this method gets the warp on the loom without cutting the cross. The warp is spread through the reed—the same reed used in the weaving—substituting for a raddle, for a more even distribution of the ends. The back loop of the cross is retained and eventually slipped onto the back tie rod, distributed evenly in preparation for beaming. The tension, so carefully maintained during winding, is never disturbed so there is little risk of tangling as the warp is beamed.

1. Find the center point of the shafts and push the heddles to each side. On a countermarch loom, it is possible to secure the upper jacks with the stabilizing pins and lower the whole unit. Rest the shafts and pinned upper jacks on the sides of the loom above the knee beam (Figure 1).

2. Remove the reed and top of the beater. On a countermarch loom, remove the reed and allow the beater cap to slide down.

3. Insert the lease sticks into the cross, one on either side, and secure with ties (Figure 2).

4. Place two support rods through the shafts so that the ends of the rods rest on the breast and back beams. On a countermarch loom, the rods rest on the beater and back beam.

5. Lay the warp chain through, or over, the shafts and drape it over the beater at the front of the loom.

FIGURE 1

FIGURE 2

6. Tie the lease sticks perpendicular to the support rods at the back of the loom (Figure 3).

FIGURE 3

7. Place the reed on the support rods between the lease sticks and back beam.

8. Measure the reed and place the warp so that it will be centered. *Do not cut the cross* (Figure 4)*!*

FIGURE 4

9. Insert the reed hook through the reed, from the bottom up, in the dent marking the right-hand side of the web. Pull the first loop

of the warp downward through the reed. Because this warp is wound eight ends at once, they are sleyed, in bulk, through a more open reed. Four loops (eight ends) are pulled through the first dent, then three dents are skipped. The warp will eventually be sleyed in a 12-dent reed, 2 ends per dent. This spaces the warp proportionately (Figure 5) across the reed. You will resley the reed later (see Tying On, page 31) following the warp color order.

FIGURE 5

10. Turn the reed over on top of the lease sticks (Figure 6).

FIGURE 6

FIGURE 7

FIGURE 8

FIGURE 9

11. Picking up several loops at a time, pull straight up and snap to create a shed. The lease stick closest to the back beam will be visible through the reed. This snapping opens the original loop formed while winding the warp (Figure 7).

12. Divide the warp proportionately into segments the size of the space between the ropes or tapes, transfer the loops to the tie-rod, and center them between the ropes or tapes of the warp beam (Figure 8).

13. It is essential that the warp be beamed under tension. Find an assistant to hold the warp at the front of the loom under tension, or if no assistant is available, hang full water bottles on the warp to tension it. I generally use four 2-liter bottles full of water weighing a total of about 17 pounds. Divide the warp into four sections and tie a half hitch slipknot with the warp groups about 10" from the back beam. Insert one end of an S-hook in the slipknot loop and the other end to a string connected to the bottle. Position the bottles as close to the floor as possible and wind the warp onto the beam. As the warp is wound on, the bottles rise up and need to be moved back down near the floor. You may need more bottles for a wider or more closely sett warp (Figure 9).

14. Remove the support rods. The reed will now hang vertically. Suspend the reed from two cords from an above beam or tie the reed to the shaft for support (Figure 10).

15. Wind the warp on the beam, inserting paper (not corrugated paper) or one thin wind-in stick with every revolution (Figure 11).

FIGURE 10

FIGURE 11

FIGURE 12

16. Move the cross from in front of the reed to behind the reed. Carefully untie the lease sticks from each other. Starting with the lease stick closest to the reed, turn it on edge and slide it toward the reed. This opens the first shed *through* the reed (Figure 12).

Insert an extra stick into the open shed between the reed and the back beam. Pull out the lease stick that opened this shed. Turn the extra stick on edge and insert the first lease stick on top of it. Remove the extra stick. Repeat the above procedure for the second lease stick. In a dense warp, you may need to pull the shed or cross open with your hands. Tie the lease sticks together and allow them to float between the breast beam and the reed (Figure 13).

FIGURE 13

17. Continue to beam the warp. Exert tension on the warp with your hands or the water bottles, and untie the cinch and bow ties from the warp chain as it advances.

18. As the warp is wound onto the warp beam, keep the lease sticks and reed pushed as close to the shafts as possible.

19. Continue winding until the end of the warp chain is even with the breast beam. Stop.

20. Trim the ends of the warp chain evenly. This is the first time that the warp is *cut*.

21. Do not pull the warp out of the lease sticks, but leave the warp untied so that you can remove it from the reed only. In sections 2"–3"wide, pull the warp ends out of the reed and tie the sections in overhand slipknots several inches from the ends.

22. Before moving on to the next step, check the number of heddles you need on each shaft for your project. For the projects in this book, the number of heddles needed per shaft is designated in the right column of the profile draft. This number matches the same number of warp ends in the warp color order chart. Move heddles between the shafts *before* you start threading.

23. Tie the lease sticks securely to the shafts. Begin threading the heddles according to the pattern.

Threading the Blocks

The threading for each project is represented by a profile draft—a shorthand for a threading order for blocks. Each block has a specific threading order (see below) and the number of warp ends per block varies in the project drafts. The warp color order chart shows the color order for winding as well as the actual ends there are per block in the profile draft. Every time a block changes in the profile draft, the column color changes from gray to white or vice versa. The most important thing to remember is that each block has two faces or colors—pattern and background. Designate one face as pattern, the other background. Once the blocks are threaded, you're ready to move on.

Here are the threading orders for each combination of blocks and shafts used in this book and that you'll need for designing your own projects.

Four Blocks on Four Shafts

When the number of blocks equals the number of shafts, two blocks must be threaded on the same pair of adjacent shafts but in the opposite order. Every shed will contain two pattern and two background blocks.

- Thread the pattern of Block A on shaft 1, background on 2.

- Thread the pattern of Block B on shaft 3, background on 4.

- Thread the pattern of Block C on shaft 2, background on 1.

- Thread the pattern of Block D on shaft 4, background on 3.

Four Blocks on Eight Shafts

When the number of shafts is twice the number of blocks, each block is threaded on a separate pair of adjacent shafts, allowing each block to be woven independently or combined as desired. Each shed will contain a total of four blocks; each combination will be different.

- Thread the pattern of Block A on shaft 1, background on 2.

- Thread the pattern of Block B on shaft 3, background on 4.

- Thread the pattern of Block C on shaft 5, background on 6.

- Thread the pattern of Block D on shaft 7, background on 8.

Eight Blocks on Eight Shafts

When threading eight blocks on eight shafts, four of the blocks reverse in the threading order so that while ABCD are weaving pattern, EFGH automatically weave the background color. Four pattern blocks combine in every shed with four background blocks.

- Thread the pattern of Block A on shaft 1, background on 2.

- Thread the pattern of Block B on shaft 3, background on 4.

- Thread the pattern of Block C on shaft 5, background on 6.

- Thread the pattern of Block D on shaft 7, background on 8.

- Thread the pattern of Block E on shaft 2, background on 1.

- Thread the pattern of Block F on shaft 4, background on 3.

- Thread the pattern of Block G on shaft 6, background on 5.

- Thread the pattern of Block H on shaft 8, background on 7.

THREADING THE CONSTANTS

Thread the constants (see page 50) on a pair of adjacent shafts with the fewest threads. It is not necessary to thread them symmetrically; for instance, you can thread a constant on shafts 1 and 2 on the right side of the weaving and on shafts 3 and 4 on the left. In the multi-shaft designs presented in this book, constants are threaded arbitrarily on shafts 7 and 8.

Tying On

Place the reed into the beater and replace the beater cap if you removed it before threading. Find the center of the reed and measure so that the warp is centered (Figure 1). The reed will be sleyed according to the warp color order. Tie the ends again with overhand slipknots.

FIGURE 1

FIGURE 2

Unroll the apron or ropes that lie around the cloth beam to their full length. Adjust the cords for even tension. Untie the center group of warp ends and pass them around the front tie-rod to determine if you have pulled the warp through the reed far enough to tie a square knot (Figure 2).

Starting in the center of the warp, select a 1" group of threads and work any excess slack toward you until the tension is even. When tying on, it is the *right* half of the warp group that does the work. Divide the group in half and pass the right half under the tie-rod. The left half remains in the upper position. Pass the right half up and over the left half to tie the first half of a square knot. Pull taut (Figure 3). Repeat by passing the right half around the left again and pull slightly upward on the right half until the knot shifts slightly, locking the

FIGURE 3

tie. Don't pull the warp as tight as the weaving tension as the warp threads may break at the knot (Figure 4). Tie a ½" section of

FIGURE 4

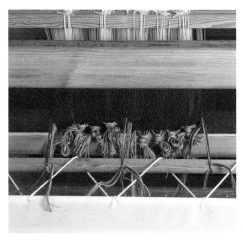

FIGURE 5

FIGURE 6

selvedge threads on one side and then a ½" section on the other side; the tie-rod should now be horizontal (Figure 5). Continue tying 1" sections for the remainder of the warp, working in toward the center until you have tied half knots in all of the warp ends. Check the tension of each section from the front and/or rear of the loom; adjust if necessary by holding the right and left halves of each tie and pulling in opposite directions and back until the half knot locks. When the tension is even, lay the left-hand threads over the right and complete the square knot (Figure 6).

Leveling Cord

After you have tied the warp to the front tie-rod, you will notice a space between the upper and lower layer of warp threads. This must be leveled before weaving begins. Cut a strong cord 12" longer than the width of the tie-rod. If the tie-rod has a hole drilled near each end, tie one end of the cord through one of these holes, weave the other end of the cord across the warp over each raised group and under each lowered group (Figure 1). At the opposite end of the tie-rod, pull the cord tight and tie it through the second hole in the tie-rod. If it has no holes, tie the cord around the tie-rod. Pull the beater against the leveling cord to begin spreading the warp to the width in reed (Figure 2). The warp will be level and ready to spread by weaving a few picks of weft, which is explained in Weaving the Elastic Heading (page 38).

FIGURE 1

FIGURE 2

Tie-Up and Treadling

A complete weaving draft—threading, tie-up, and treadle draft—accompanies each project. Read through each project's Project Notes before tying the treadles. A 4-shaft tie-up is used for weaving all 3-block, 4-shaft and all 4-block, 4-shaft patterns. Eight treadles are required for 6-block, 8-shaft patterns. Eight-block patterns threaded on eight shafts give the greatest number of tie-up combinations. The tie-ups used in this book are shown with the treadles in adjacent pairs. In the treadling, a black square represents the thick pick; a square with a slash, the thin pick. Throw the thick pick first.

Beginners often find writing the tie-up draft the most difficult aspect of rep weave. A tie-up draft exercise is given in Designing with Blocks (page 51). Follow this procedure to make the task as easy as possible.

Weaving

or me, the anticipation of what will unfold as I weave is the reason I weave rep. It's wonderfully exciting. During what I call "incubator time," I start with a mental picture of the end result. Picking and blending warp colors, selecting the fabric weft, winding the warp, dressing the loom, and threading are all parts of the design procedure. Even though I think I know how my design will turn out, I'm always surprised at the possibilities presented each time I step on a treadle. There are a lot of "what ifs." I like to keep an open mind and be flexible; if I don't like what I've woven, I unweave and try again. It's a good lesson in humility.

But before you can weave a single pick, you'll need to prepare your weft materials.

Weft Preparation

Wefts suitable for weaving rep include fabric, rug filler, mop cotton, string yarn, or any number of other fibers. In fact, you can use just about anything, but your choice is always based on the end use of the item. How much weft you'll need is not always easy to estimate because of the wide variety of wefts that can be used. Weave a sample first; this will help you calculate how much weft you need for the actual project. Weigh different types of fibers and record the amounts used for future projects. Note fiber yardages along with weights and the amount needed to weave a given piece. Record this information. The more certain you are as to how far a pound of fiber or fabric will go, the better prepared you will be to purchase the correct amount needed to weave a project using that fiber or fabric as weft.

I've weighed many kinds of fabrics. For example, 1 yard of cotton calico 45" wide weighs about 4³/₄ ounces. A placemat measuring 12" × 18" requires 1¹/₂ yards (about 7 ounces) of fabric, cut into strips 1" wide, doubled on the shuttle. To weave eight placemats, you'll need 12 yards of fabric. Drapery-weight 100% cotton fabric 54" wide weighs about 7½ ounces per yard. You'll need 1 yard of this fabric to weave a 12" × 18" placemat.

If fabric needs to be washed, do so before cutting the fabric. Washing removes sizing from the fabric (material that hasn't been sized may not need to be washed). I have found that better quality fabric doesn't have as much sizing as lower-grade fabrics. If you do wash it, use tepid water and regular detergent, rinse well, hang to dry, and press if needed. Machine washing is not recommended for yardages longer than 7 to 8 yards.

Cutting the Fabric

Setting up a work area for each task will make the job easier and more efficient. The amount of fabric required to weave a given project can influence your preparation method. For example, a full bolt of fabric is cumbersome to handle.

Cut the fabric into strips with the grain of the fabric parallel to the selvedge (straight grain is more stable than cross grain). The greater the length of the fabric strip, the faster the preparation. Your can use various cutting tools such as a cloth stripping machine, rotary cutter, or scissors.

To get the fabric into manageable pieces, I use a self-healing cutting mat, rotary cutting tool, and a plastic ruler 5" wide that is made especially for rotary cutting. Place the mat on a table and on it lay the fabric, folded selvedge to selvedge. Place the ruler on the fabric and cut off the woven selvedge the length of the ruler (Figure 1). Reposition the ruler along the newly cut edge and cut strips, with the grain of the fabric, the width of the ruler (Figure 2). Pull the fabric toward yourself and continue each cut. Cut the entire length of fabric. Fold

FIGURE 1

FIGURE 2

FIGURE 3

FIGURE 4

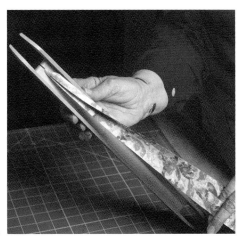

FIGURE 5

each fabric strip and put aside (Figure 3). Now position one of the strips on the cutting mat and recut it into strips 1" wide (Figure 4). Place the back of one 1" strip against the face of a second strip and wind them together onto a rug, rag, or stick shuttle (Figure 5). This method prevents the wrong side of the fabric from showing if the strips shift out of alignment during weaving.

Filler or Roving

Roving and rug fillers make suitable wefts although they don't provide the same hand or visual impact as printed fabrics. Maysville rug roping, rug filler, and mop cotton can all be used for weft in rep weave. 100% cotton rug roping is available in a limited color range and Maysville 100% cotton rug filler, in a wider color range. You do not need to wash these yarns before weaving. Mop cotton—a cord made up of miscellaneous fibers—is available only in a natural color. Take-up and shrinkage will vary depending on which of these wefts you use, so you will need to recalculate the weft amount needed when changing from one weft material to another.

Headings

Weaving a heading is the first step when beginning a project and the last step before cutting the completed weaving off the loom. The heading maintains compression in the weave, holds the woven portion of the rug from unweaving, and is a transition between the weaving and the edge. Headings, like fringes or hems, are meant to complement and enhance, not detract from the weaving. A properly woven heading should be as wide as the finished weaving. Nothing looks worse than a skimpy, misshapen, puckered heading that won't lie flat or one that is too loosely woven and wider than need be. Weaving headings takes time and consideration to ensure proper fit.

During weaving, the warp is kept under tight tension, and the more open the sett, the greater the potential for draw-in. An elastic heading (see page 39) is the solution as it can stretch and adjust to the width of the weaving, no matter which weft is used in the body of the weave.

Before I start the heading, I check to see if the color order and placement of warp threads are correct. If I have to move and rethread warps after threading is complete, I remove the lease sticks and reinsert them after any threading change to keep the warp absolutely straight from the shafts to the back beam. If that distance is short on your loom, loosen the tension and slip the lease sticks over the back beam. They will hang above the warp beam and be out of the way (Figure 1). Every time you advance the warp, straighten and untangle the threads before you resume weaving.

The heading forms a solid web to beat against and holds the weaving in place. In rep weave, I use the same thread that I use in the warp to weave the heading. For these projects, it's 8/4 carpet warp. Choose a color of carpet warp for the heading that matches or

FIGURE 1

complements the weft. The amount of weft needed to weave a firm heading varies according to the density of the sett. Headings are woven in plain weave, and every pair of adjacent treadles ties up to plain weave in different block combinations. The same pair of treadles that weaves the first thick pick—the pattern block—is used to make a smooth transition between the heading and weaving. If a different pair of treadles has been used to weave the heading, there will be a common block in which the thick and thin picks of wefts lie in the same shed making it look like a mistake (see page 50 for ways to avoid this.)

Because the thick pattern weft is generally straight-grain fabric or a cordlike fiber,
it is not likely to stretch or shrink during or
after weaving. Therefore, the heading must
be woven to fit and accommodate the width
of the weaving as it will appear on the loom
without shrinkage and draw-in, but it should
not contain an excess of weft, which could
cause the heading to ripple.

Weaving the Elastic Heading

Prepare a quill of 8/4 cotton carpet warp for a
boat shuttle and, without beating, throw three
picks in the tabby sheds, leaving a small loop
of weft at each selvedge. Close the shed and
beat (Figure 1 and Figure 2). This method
spreads the warp before beginning the elastic
heading. It closes the gaps in the web created
by tying knots to the tie-rod. If necessary, weave
a few more picks until the warp is distributed
evenly. Then begin the elastic heading:

Throw the weft just once and, with the
shed open, insert one index finger so there is
a loop at the selvedge edge (Figure 3). With
the shuttle in your other hand, place the
thumb of that hand lightly on the bobbin to

FIGURE 2

FIGURE 3

FIGURE 1

FIGURE 4

FIGURE 5

FIGURE 6

FIGURE 7

keep it from unwinding. Pull the end of the weft attached to the shuttle until it is snug around your finger and use your middle finger to support the web from underneath (Figure 4). The pressure from below helps control the amount of draw-in on the weft. Remove your index finger from the loop and set the weft at the selvedge by flicking it into the shed with your index finger. With the same finger, lift the weft near the center of the shed about 1½" above the fell line. With your other hand (holding the shuttle), pull the open end of the weft down to the fell line to create an inverted V (Figure 5). Change and beat on the *opposite* shed. Notice that the reed hits the top of the inverted V and distributes the excess weft evenly across the width of the web (Figure 6). Repeat the procedure and beat in slow motion to observe how effectively this method works. Use both hands to pull the selvedges in opposite directions to feel the stretch (Figure 7). These five words sum up the steps needed to weave an elastic heading: throw, set, invert, change, beat. Elasticity is created only when the weft is beaten on the opposite shed.

To prove the point, throw another shot of weft and use the same procedure to make the inverted V but beat with an *open* shed. Notice that the excess weft so carefully pulled into the inverted V repositioned itself and created two loops about 2" from each selvedge. Repeat the procedure but this time beat on a *flat* (closed) shed. The excess weft makes a loop near the center of the web. Neither of these last two methods distributes the weft nor creates elasticity in the heading.

The depth of the inverted V depends on the warp sett and the width in reed. In general, the closer the sett, the lower you should make the inverted V. If the inverted V is too high, too much weft will be distributed across the weft, causing rippling from side to side. A very closely sett warp requires that the weft be thrown straight across the web with little or no excess, pulled taut, and beaten on the opposite shed. Check the width in the reed every time the beater strikes the web. You will maintain the exact width in the reed if you pay close attention when the reed is against the web, not when the beater is resting.

Hems

An elongated heading can be used as a hem and is the perfect finish for placemats, table runners, and rugs when a fringe is not desired or necessary. Follow the procedure described above, allowing a woven length of about $1^3/_4$"—roughly 20 picks— to make a triple-folded hem that brings the first fold to the edge of the first thick pick so the entire head-ing becomes the hem. Hand- or machine-stitch the folded hem.

As you weave the hem, check the width in the reed every time the beater strikes the web. An elastic hem can be stretched to match the width of the weaving as you finish it, but it's better to do it right from the start.

Interlocking Wefts at Selvedge

It is imperative that the alternating thick and thin weft picks interlock at the selvedge. A floating selvedge is not used or necessary. After weaving the elastic heading, leave the shuttle at the selvedge edge and weave the first thick weft, taper the end, wrap the selvedge, and tuck the tail into the same shed. The initial pick of thin weft must follow in the same direction as the thick pick, but in the opposite shed.

The importance of starting correctly eliminates problems later on. Specifically, every time the thin pick is omitted—when the tie-down shed happens to be the next pattern shed—the weft order is altered. The thin pick still follows the thick pick but travels in the opposite direction. When the thin pick is omitted again, at the next block change, the original order is restored. If the shuttles travel in opposite directions from the beginning, you will have trouble inter-locking the wefts.

Two rules apply when using two wefts, especially when the thick weft is fabric. These rules will help you understand not only how the wefts interlock but how the thick weft folds and turns around the selvedge. When both the thick and thin wefts are woven to the same side of the web, open the new shed and throw the thick weft. Before pulling the loop of the thick weft closed, look at the wefts in relationship to the selvedge. It is the thin weft that indicates how the rule applies. For the two wefts to interlock so that the selvedge thread is not left unwoven, the following must take place:

First rule: Interlock. When the thin weft lies over the last selvedge thread, the thin weft weaves under the thick weft. When the thin weft lies under the last selvedge thread, it weaves over the thick weft. It's the familiar weaving mantra, over-under and under-over. It helps to speak the rules aloud while performing the task.

Second rule: Turning the thick (fabric) weft. On the new shed, when the last selvedge thread is raised, fold the thick weft down (under) and weave into the shed. Or, on the new shed, when the last selvedge thread is down, fold the thick weft up (over) and weave into the shed. Observe that the thick fabric weft enters the web further according to the position of the last selvedge thread. This procedure creates continuity along the selvedge edge.

Here's an example of the second rule applied: Begin with the thick weft and throw the shuttle from the same side of the web where the last thin weft exited. If the thick weft is fabric, the two strips should lie flat, one atop the other and wrong side up. Fold the fabric by pulling it taut with a hand on either side of the web so that the wrong side is folded inward (Figure 1). Look at the last selvedge thread on the side of the loom where the fabric turns. If the last selvedge thread is raised, fold the fabric down (under) (Figure 2). If the last selvedge

FIGURE 1

FIGURE 2

FIGURE 3

FIGURE 4

FIGURE 5

thread is down, fold the fabric up (over) (Figure 3). With a finger in the loop of the folded fabric, position the turn so that it extends at least two dents beyond the last selvedge, remove your finger, and draw the folded edge down to the fell line (Figure 4). The folded edge of the fabric always faces the weaver. If the fold faces away, it may turn over when beaten. Close the shed and beat.

While you were busy turning the fabric, the previous pick of thin thread may have worked loose. Pull the thin weft gently, just enough to pull out the slack before throwing the shuttle (Figure 5). Make an inverted V and beat on the opposite shed. Check the width in reed every time the beater strikes the web. Each folded turn of the fabric extends two dents beyond the selvedge. If you are consistent, the selvedge edges will be straight with no draw-in, and the thick picks will be beaten tightly together. This procedure takes some getting used to, but once accomplished, the weaving will progress quickly. Review the rules for interlocking two wefts and turning at the selvedge.

Beating

Ineffective beating can result in a loosely woven runner or placemat, but factors other than beating must be taken into consideration when alternating wefts of different sizes. The position of the fell line in relation to the beater and the angle at which the reed strikes the web are critical. Ideally, the fell line should remain halfway between the beater at rest and the breast beam. Therefore, the warp must be advanced frequently to maintain the angle of the beat. To achieve the most efficient packing, the reed must strike the web at an angle greater than 90°. By making the inverted V on the thin weft (see page 40), the extra weft is distributed along the fell line, allowing the thick wefts to pack more closely together than they otherwise would, resulting in a more compact, tightly woven piece. If the thick wefts cannot be beaten all the way to the fell line, the weft will be loosely packed. Remember to beat the thick weft on a flat (closed) shed and make the inverted V with the thin weft and beat it on the opposite shed.

The beat on jack looms generally is at an angle less than 90° when the shafts are at rest, making packing less effective. Raising all of the shafts increases the angle of the warp in relation to the reed and greatly improves beating quality. All shafts rise together when any pair of adjacent treadles is pressed because treadles are tied to opposite odd or even shafts.

On a countermarch loom, an overhead beater swings from a beater cradle, which allows the beater to be moved forward or backward to maintain the correct beating angle. The beater is positioned in the front notch of the cradle when weaving begins so that it strikes the web at an angle greater than 90°. During weaving, as the distance between the fell line and the beater decreases, the beater is moved back to the next position in the cradle to maintain the angle of the beat at the fell line. Moving the beater in the cradle also eliminates the need to advance the warp as frequently. When the beater reaches the back notch of the cradle and the shed diminishes, the warp is once again advanced. If you are weaving very wide cloth and/or are using more than four shafts, it may be easier to advance the warp more frequently rather than move the beater in the cradle.

Tensioning the Warp

Rep weave demands a tight tension during all stages of production—beaming, weaving, and even resting. After the warp has been tied to the tie-rod and tensioned for weaving, the tension must remain constant. Why calculate the critical final lengths of a woven piece if the tension will fluctuate as it is woven? Not that you must use all your strength to tighten the warp as much as you can: a tight tension that can be reproduced every time the warp is advanced will be sufficient.

An important note about advancing the warp: Release tension on the cloth beam before releasing the warp beam, whether your loom has a brake-release pedal or a ratchet-and-pawl assembly. Attempting to release the warp beam while it is under tension is ill-advised and may cause your carefully beamed warp to unwind onto the floor. To avoid damaging loom parts, release the tension on both the cloth beam and the warp beam before advancing the warp.

Another important note: Don't release the tension on the warp when you're done weaving for the day; otherwise, you'll never be able to get an accurate length measurement. When you start a project, stay with it and complete it as soon as possible. If you plan to weave several pieces, such as placemats, complete one to the end and weave the heading. Under tension, take and record the measurement from the first thick pick to the last one. Count the number of picks in a single placemat. Measure 3" on the weaving and count the picks in that distance. Then measure 6" and count the picks. Depending on how many thin wefts you have omitted, the count may change. Don't assume that the measurements will remain the same when you omit a few thin picks, they won't! Careful measurements insure that all placemats are the same size. Always loosen the tension before cutting the warp at the back tie-rod.

Adjusting from Front and Rear

The solution to an improperly tensioned warp is to tighten the cloth beam and then make the final adjustment from the rear of the loom on the warp beam; doing this eliminates excess slack in both directions, creates a larger shed, and properly tensions the warp. By contrast, tightening only from the cloth beam, particularly on a jack loom, greatly diminishes the shed.

Repairing Broken or Frayed Warps

What to do when you encounter a broken or frayed warp thread depends on where the break occurs. When to repair the thread depends on whether you are weaving a single piece or a series on the same warp. If the break occurs at the fell line, it is best to add a replacement thread weighted off the back beam and long enough to wrap around a T-pin inserted in the woven fabric for needle weaving after you have reached the end of the current weaving. At this point, you can tie the far end of the replacement thread to the original warp end with a weaver's knot, as shown. If the broken thread occurs in a run of placemats, follow the procedure above

but make the replacement thread long enough that you can pull it through the partially woven mat with a crochet hook or long blunt-end needle so that the break falls at the cutting line between mats.

To repair a broken or frayed thread in the shaft, isolate both ends of the broken thread and lay them at an angle across the warp for greater visibility. Tie a weaver's knot, trim, and glue; or pull the near end of the broken end onto the woven fabric, pin, and wrap enough to thread on a needle and later sew back into the weaving as far as the beginning of the heading around the pin. Cut a replacement thread long enough that you can wrap one end around the same pin, rethread the other end through the shaft, and tie with a bowknot to the rest of the original end at the stretch beam. As the bowknot advances toward the shaft, untie and reposition the new bowknot at the back beam.

Frayed ends must be cut and replaced as above or glued to reduce further fraying. Use a drop of flexible fabric glue to smooth loose ends; allow it to dry before continuing to weave.

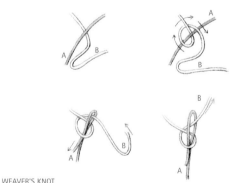

WEAVER'S KNOT

Tensioning Loose Threads

Selvedge threads do not become loose because we touch them. Unlike the other warp ends, which are constantly moving up and down to accommodate the wefts, selvedge threads lie in a straight vertical line and float in the fold of the wefts. Selvedge ends that are loose need to be adjusted to match the tension of the rest of the warp. A perfect place to remove excess slack in selvedges is at the beginning of a new mat. Squeeze the selvedge threads between your index finger and thumb and pull them toward yourself to test the tension. Loose threads will buckle or bend, indicating the need to tighten the tension. Weave two picks of a different-colored weft to indicate the cutting line between the 1³/₄" headings on two placemats. On a new placemat, weave at least 1" beyond the cutting line and test the tension. If the selvedges are too loose, at the cutting line, insert a crochet hook or needle under a single selvedge end, slowly apply enough pressure to draw up the excess slack into a small loop. A correctly woven heading will hold the loops of excess selvedge securely during weaving. Tighten the remaining selvedge end as needed. Continue weaving, tightening

again as necessary. The loops will remain between headings and will be cut away when the mats are cut apart.

On a long runner or rug, work any excess slack in the selvedges from the center toward each heading, adjusting when the weaving is complete and off the loom. Adjusting the tension on selvedge threads can be done at any point during weaving, but it makes more sense to do it at the beginning or end. Take care not to pull the selvedge threads so tight that they break.

Designing with Blocks for Rep

n developing a way to design blocks and treadling drafts, I found it necessary to make some guidelines which I call "rules." You've encountered some of these already in the section on Threading the Blocks (page 29). Use these rules when designing your own rep weaves.

Rep weaves with more than two blocks require different rules for threading and modified techniques for weaving. Threading in a straight draw is no longer an option, nor are changing the block by weaving a second pick of thin weft in the opposite shed or omitting the thin weft altogether.

Rules

Rule 1: Each design block is threaded on a pair of adjacent shafts—one color on the odd shafts, the other on the even. For example, pattern is threaded on shaft 1, background on shaft 2, pattern on 3, background on 4.

Rule 2: Each block has two faces, pattern and background; therefore, each block of design requires two treadles—one to weave the pattern face and the other to weave the background face. Adjacent treadles with opposite tie-ups are treadled as follows—the first with the thick weft followed by the second with the thin weft.

Rule 3: Each block requires two treadles, and each treadle is tied with either the odd or even shaft of every block in the draft.

Rule 4: In certain designs, two blocks weave together, but the weaver can select as the second block either the block to the right or the block to the left of the main block. This is true only when the number of blocks equals the number of shafts on which the design is threaded. *Example*: A 4-block design threaded on four shafts will always produce two pattern and two background blocks per shed. When Block A is the main block, it may be combined with either Blocks B or D (and never Block C because they share the same pair of shafts).

Rule 5: When blocks are used individually or in combination, twice the number of shafts than blocks need to be used. *Example:* Threading a 4-block design on eight shafts allows greater flexibility in design in that it will produce the following sheds—a single pattern block, any two pattern blocks, three pattern blocks, all pattern, or background. Four shafts rise in every shed in different pattern and background combinations.

Rule 6: When weaving a new block combination of more than two blocks, the thick pick of one or more blocks lies in the same shed as the previous thin pick. These common blocks—one common block of the last thin pick lies in the same common shed as the new block—are unavoidable and are characteristic of rep weave. Common blocks occur only when a new pattern shed is woven and are eliminated when the same thick and thin sheds are repeated. No common blocks occur when a tie-down is omitted and replaced by the thick weft because those sheds are opposite. Every shed must be tied-down before moving to a new block combination.

Terminology

As mentioned in the Theory chapter, I've coined some terminology that further defines my use of color and blocks:

A **constant** generally is a minimum of two threads of the same color, or it may contain threads of several related colors that blend visually to give a more dynamic quality to the stripe, more than you would get with a single-color stripe. The constant is not a block. They are threaded on a pair of adjacent shafts or it shares shafts with a block that has the fewest threads, and is visible on the front and back of the weaving. A constant can be used alone or combined with other constants to create stripes or borders in the weaving. It may blend with either pattern or background threads of adjacent blocks to separate or produce larger design elements.

An **outline** is a contrasting or similar-colored thread that identifies and draws attention to the edge of a block or design area. When used to outline a block, a single thread is used at the edge or edges of the block on the same shaft as the pattern threads. Used to outline a constant, two threads of the same color are each threaded on a pair of adjacent shafts and produce a thin stripe as one or the other outline threads is visible in every shed. An outline is only a color change. They can appear on any pair of shafts, and need not be symmetrically threaded.

A **phantom block** gives the illusion of a block created by the use of color rather than threading order. A phantom block may be solid, shaded, or outlined. It may appear within the pattern threads, background threads, or both threads of any given block.

Here is the warp color order chart from the Chili Cook-Off placemats denoting the outline, constants, and phantom blocks.

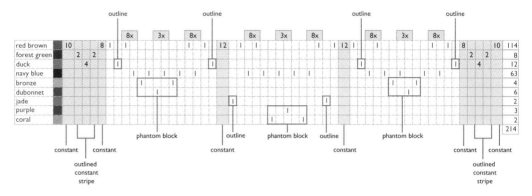

Chili Cookoff Placemats warp color order—see photo page 62

Tie-Up

In the tie-up draft shown below to illustrate how a tie-up is designed, a circle surrounding a letter in a column designates a block raised by a given treadle. An empty circle in the same column represents the background of that block.

Tie-up Draft Exercise

Beginners often find writing the tie-up draft the most difficult aspect of rep weave. Follow this procedure to make the task as easy as possible.

To draft a 4-block, 4-shaft tie-up, first draw a square grid four columns wide and four rows high.

Number the columns, from left to right, 1 through 4 to represent the treadles.

Letter the rows along the left side, from bottom to top, A, C, B, D to represent the pattern face of each block. Because a 4-block pattern is threaded in a progressing manner, the A block is threaded on shafts 1 and 2 and followed by a B block threaded on shafts 3 and 4. It becomes necessary to reverse the blocks to thread the C block on shaft 2 and 1, followed by the D block on shafts 4 and 3.

Number the rows along the right side from bottom to top to represent shafts 1 through 4.

Now follow the instructions below.

To write the tie-up draft: Start with the first two letters of the alphabet (A) and (B) and number 1. Place a 1 below the first column to represent treadle 1 and draw a circle in each of the spaces that correspond to the shafts that raise Blocks A and B. In a 4-block draft, treadle 1 must raise two blocks together. In each circle, place the letter of the block raised. Say to yourself, "Treadle 1 raises the A and B blocks."

Automatically (because adjacent treadles are tied with opposite tie-ups) draw circles in the opposite squares on the adjacent treadle 2.

Treadle 3 is next. The only other block that can rise with Block A is Block D. Draw circles on shafts 1 and 4; write the letter of each block raised in the appropriate circle. Automatically draw circles in the opposite squares on treadle 4 and insert the letters of the blocks raised, C and B. The 4-shaft tie-up is now complete. The left side of the grid is shaded to show that treadle 1 and 2 are the adjacent pair.

The first treadle of a pair weaves is the thick pick; the second treadle, the thin pick. Either treadle can be used first to weave the thick pick, followed by the other treadle with the thin pick.

Now let's draft a 3-block, 8-shaft tie-up. Each block will be threaded on a separate pair of adjacent shafts. The pattern threads of Block A are on shaft 1, and the background threads are on shaft 2. The pattern threads of Block B are on shaft 3, and the background threads are on shaft 4. The pattern threads of Block C on are on shaft 5, and the background threads are on shaft 6. Constants are threaded on shafts 7 and 8 and alternate every other shed regardless of treadling order. The tie-up draft is written to show the sequence of raising pattern first of Block A, next of Blocks A and B, and finally of Blocks A, B, and C.

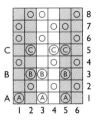

Draw a 3-block, 8-shaft, 8-treadle tie-up draft. On treadle 1, draw a circle on shaft 1 and place the letter A inside. Block A is the only pattern block on treadle 1, but three more shafts must also rise to create a tabby shed: the background of Blocks B and C and one shaft of the constant. Draw a circle on shafts 4, 6, and 7; do not letter these circles. Automatically draw circles in the opposite squares on treadle 2 and write the letter of a block only if it shows pattern. Bracket the top of the first two treadles and write the letter of the raised pattern block above each treadle—it helps eliminate duplication of tie-ups. The letters above the brackets helps you see which pattern blocks are woven on each treadle.

For treadle 3, draw circles in the squares to raise the pattern of Blocks A and B, background of C, and shaft 8, a constant. Write the letters of the raised pattern blocks only, not the background blocks. Automatically draw circles in the opposite squares on treadle 4. Write the letter of the raised blocks—in this case, pattern of Block C. Two circles are background; the third (shaft 7) is a constant. Bracket adjacent treadles and write the letters of the blocks above.

For treadle 5, draw circles in the squares that raise Blocks A, B, and C, and a constant. Letter the blocks. Automatically draw circles in the opposite squares on treadle 6. The only single pattern block not shown is Block B.

Draw a circle on treadle 7 in the square that raises shaft 3. Place the letter B in the circle. Three more shafts must rise, the background of A and C and the constant.

Continue as before drawing circles in the opposite squares on treadle 8 and write the letter of the raised blocks only.

Here are a couple of 4-block patterns on eight shafts, one with eight and the other with ten treadles.

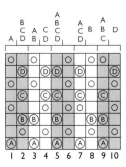

2-Block Designs

ep weave could be called a glorified log cabin—an American term for a weave structure with two blocks, two colors, and primarily, two shafts. Both structures are plain weave—log cabin, a true plain weave because the warp and weft are balanced, and rep, a derivative of plain weave because the warp threads are densely sett and sometimes doubled, even quadrupled in the heddle. They also share threading similarities—colors alternate to create blocks, and two threads of the same color are adjacent so that during weaving the blocks can change or reverse color. The last similarity is in the weaving—thick and thin weights of weft fabric and thread alternate, and blocks of color are created by changing the weft sequences.

Three projects, each for two blocks, are presented in this chapter along with information on 2-block threading variations, headings, weaving procedures, and changing blocks. Constants, outline threads, and phantom blocks will be used as the number of blocks and shafts increase. Although the threading and tie-up drafts are written for two blocks, they can also be threaded on four shafts in a straight draw—1, 2, 3, 4—alternating colors as you would on two shafts. The loom waste is calculated for a 4-shaft threading. Remember that shafts 1 and 3 rise together followed by shafts 2 and 4. Refer to Weft Preparation (page 35) for calculating how much weft will be needed and follow the Warping process (page 19).

2-Block, 2-Shaft Projects

Checkerboard Placemats

Designs need not be complicated. A simple 2-block pattern with blocks of different sizes makes a pleasing design. Here, two colors in a medium and dark value—forest and copper—are used for the warp, and a printed calico in a medium value is used as the weft to create an interesting, rich-toned placemat. Since the values of the two warp colors are similar, I designated forest as the pattern and copper as the background. The interaction of warp and weft makes the colors of the warp appear to be different after weaving—forest appears black and copper appears rust-red.

PROJECT NOTES

Warp Maysville 8/4 cotton carpet warp in two colors: forest green #12 (473 yd), copper #35 (473 yd)

Thick Weft Two 1" strips of calico fabric, the front of one strip wound to the back of the other strip on a rag shuttle

Thin Weft Maysville 8/4 cotton carpet warp in a color to match the fabric

Warp Sett 20 ends per inch, 1 thread per heddle

Reed 10 dent, sleyed 2 ends per dent

Width in Reed 12½"

Finished Width Same or slightly wider, measured at the fold of the fabric

Total Ends 252

Number of Placemats Four

Cloth Length Four placemats, each finished to 18¼"

Raw Length Each placemat woven under tension to 22"

Take-Up 17% (during weaving) 12½"

Shrinkage 17% (after weaving) 12½"

Tie-On 8"

Hems 1¾" × 8 edges = 14"

Loom Waste 16" (4" per shaft)

Total Warp Length 136" or 3¾ yards

WARP COLOR ORDER

Wind a 3¾-yard warp with the two designated warp colors—126 ends of forest and 126 ends of copper—holding one end of each color and placing a finger between threads. After winding the warp, follow the directions for Warping the Loom (page 25).

THREADING

This 2-block profile is threaded on two shafts. Each block in a profile draft represents a specified number of warp ends: Blocks A and B alternate and contain either 32 or 12 ends per block. Thread the pattern of Block A on shaft 1, alternated with background on shaft 2. (The background color is designated by a slash.) Thread the pattern of Block B on shaft 2, alternated with background on shaft 1. Thread the shafts the number of times indicated on the draft. Note that two threads of the same color are adjacent where the blocks change. For example, the threading begins with forest, copper, repeated eight times and then becomes copper, forest, repeated three times.

TIE-UP

Each shaft is tied to a separate treadle. The first treadle weaves the thick weft—the calico

forest green		126
copper		126
		252

warp color order

threading

fabric—followed by the second treadle with the thin weft—carpet warp.

WEAVING

Spread the warp to the width of the reed by weaving 6–8 picks of 8/4 cotton weft. Follow the directions for Weaving an Elastic Heading (page 38). Do not cut the weft but leave the

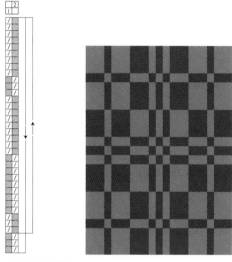

tie-up and treadling

shuttle at the right selvedge because you will use it again for the thin weft. Weave the thick weft to the left, taper the end, wrap the selvedge, tuck the tail into the same shed, close the shed and beat. Follow with the thin weft in the same direction on the opposite shed of the thick weft, change shed and beat. Since this placemat is 12½" wide and the desired finished length is 18¼" plus hems, each block must be made longer than its finished length when woven to obtain the correct total length, which under tension is about 22". Weave the blocks as drawn in, that is, in the same order in which they are threaded.

Start keeping track of the number of thick and thin picks woven per inch when the warp is under tension. That number is about 3 thick and 3 thin picks but will vary according to the type of loom, warp tension, beating, and thick weft used. The first block in the threading draft contains 32 warp ends—16 forest, 16 copper—making the block about 1½" wide in the reed. The block, once it's off the loom, should appear to be woven "square," that is, as high as the block is wide. But due to shrinkage, the block needs to be woven longer—four or five picks of thick weft will probably be sufficient. Plan and weave half the mat (11") under tension, then check your measurements. You may need to unweave part of what you have woven if adjustments are necessary.

To elongate the block, weave the first block with 9 picks of thick weft, each tied down with a thin pick. To change blocks, either (1) omit the thin pick of the old block, causing 2 thick picks to lie side by side, or (2) throw a second pick of thin weft, counting as the first pick of the new block, which automatically reverses the blocks.

Weave the second, which is narrow, with 3 picks of thick weft. Follow the block order in the profile draft and weave each wide block with 9 picks, each narrow block with 3. Assuming that the above estimated measurements are accurate, you'll need 69 picks each of thick and thin weft to weave the placemat. But 69 picks divided by 3 picks per inch equals 23", a little longer than the correct woven length under tension.

Using the first method when changing blocks, omitting the thin picks between block changes altogether results in a slightly shorter length. (Keeping notes is essential to help you decide which method works best for you.) Here's another option—weave the wide blocks with 8 thick picks and the narrow blocks with 4 thick picks, making a total of 68 picks. On the other hand, the blocks have more pleasing proportions if the narrow blocks are woven with 3 picks; you decide.

In summary, a placemat requires 66–70 picks each of thick and thin wefts. This measurement is based on the way I weave, however. You must establish and record your own measurements. Always measure under tension and remember that once the weaving is off the loom and relaxed, shrinkage will reduce the length by as much as 17%. The finished weaving should match the cloth length in the original project plan.

FINISHING

Make triple-folded hems, following the directions for Headings and Hems (page 140).

Chili Cook-Off Placemats

Chili cook-offs are common in the Southwest. They may be as small as a rivalry between families or friends or as large as a regional or statewide competition. The varieties of chili itself are even greater. My favorite chili recipe comes from Santa Clara Pueblo; its deep red color inspired this project.

In the Checkerboard Placemats, the design blocks connect at the corners. In this 2-block design, three new elements are added—a constant, an outline thread, and a phantom block—as diagrammed in the Designing with Blocks chapter (page 49). The constants form stripes and background that separate and create space around the blocks, resulting in an open, simpler design. Eight constants run lengthwise through the weaving, two of which form stripes parallel to each selvedge. An outline thread enlivens the surface and makes the design more interesting. The outline thread, although of a different color, belongs to the same block that it edges. Phantom blocks are part of the background. They contain different colors and in this case are outlined with threads that make them even more apparent. The phantom blocks connect the midsections of large blocks in three vertical columns. The addition of these new elements in this 2-block design adds visual interest and complexity.

PROJECT NOTES

Warp Maysville 8/4 cotton carpet warp in the following colors:

Background: red brown #7 (428 yd)

Pattern: forest green #12 (38 yd), duck #47 (45 yd), navy blue #5 (236 yd), dubonnet #71 (23 yd), purple #25 (12 yd)

Outline: duck #47 (45 yd), bronze #40 (15 yd), jade #37 (8 yd)

Thick Weft Two 1" strips of calico fabric, the front of one strip wound to the back of the other strip on a rag shuttle

Thin Weft Maysville 8/4 cotton carpet warp in a color to match the fabric

Warp Sett 16 ends per inch, 1 thread per heddle

Reed 8 dent, sleyed 2 ends per dent

Width in Reed 13"

Finished Width Same or slightly wider, measured at the fold of the fabric

Total Ends 214, including 4 extra selvedge threads

Number of Placemats Four

Follow the Cloth Length through Warp Length as in the Checkerboard Placemats.

WARP COLOR ORDER

Follow the warp color order from left to right and wind a $3^3/_4$-yard warp, two threads at a time. The first and last groups of brown warp

		8x		3x		8x			8x		3x		8x			8x		3x		8x		
red brown	10		8	I		I		I	I	12	I		I		I	I	12	I		I		I	I	8		10	114
forest green		2	2					I				I				I				2	2		10
duck			4		I			I				I				I				4		12
navy blue				I	I	I	I	I		I	I	I	I	I		I	I	I	I	I	I		63
bronze					I		I				I	I			4
dubonnet						I				I				I		6
jade							I		I			2
purple								I		I		I		3
																							214

warp color order

threading

contain 10 ends each—8 plus 2 extra selvedge threads. A number by itself indicates a constant. When changing colors, simply splice the ends of the old and new colors together (see Splicing, page 20) and continue. After winding the warp, follow the directions for Warping the Loom (page 25).

THREADING

The threads from the lease sticks are in the proper threading sequence although it may be necessary to switch the color order of the two threads when the blocks change. Thread each of the first two heddles with two threads of the same color and sley all four ends in the same dent at each selvedge. Because of the open sett, the tendency of the warp to draw in is great; doubling the selvedge helps maintain the width in the reed. Thread alternately on two shafts directly from the profile draft. Pay close attention to the outline threads along the edges of large Blocks A and B as well as

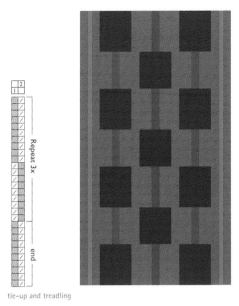

Repeat 3x

end

tie-up and treadling

to the change of colors in the background that creates the illusion of another block—the phantom block.

TIE-UP

Each shaft is tied to a separate treadle. The first treadle weaves the thick weft—the calico fabric—followed by the second treadle with the thin weft—carpet warp.

WEAVING

Spread the warp to the width of the reed by weaving 6–8 picks of 8/4 cotton. Following the directions for Weaving an Elastic Heading (page 38), weave a 1³/₄" elastic heading with the 8/4 weft, about 20 picks, before introducing the first thick fabric weft. Begin the thick weft, taper the end, wrap the selvedge, tuck the tail into the same shed, and beat. Experiment with the two methods used for changing blocks (see page 58) and weave at least 6" before you decide which method you will use. Pay attention to the feel of the beat as well as the sound of the beater striking the web. Pick the method that best packs the thick picks and controls the width-in-reed. Now unweave to the heading and begin again. Throw the thick weft and follow in the same direction on the opposite shed with the thin weft. Alternate weaving thick and thin wefts to the desired length and change blocks. Follow the treadling draft to the end.

FINISHING

Make triple-folded hems, following the directions for Headings and Hems (page 140).

Vermilion Cliffs Placemats

The Vermilion Cliffs rise spectacularly northeast of the Grand Canyon and north-west of the Colorado River. The bands of colorful sedimentary rock include Permian Kaibab Limestone at the bottom with layers of Triassic and Jurassic rocks above. The colors vary from the blue, gray, and purple of the Chinle Formation shales to the pale salmon of the Navajo Sandstone with brown, red, tan, and white bands that change color as the light changes. John Wesley Powell, a Civil War veteran and the second director of the United States Geological Survey, named the cliffs. Zane Grey was so impressed with the Vermilion Cliffs that he described them in his novel *Heritage of the Desert* (1910).

In these mats, the constant works with the blocks to make them appear wider. Two pattern blocks, one on either side of the constant, are the same color as the constant although each block occupies a different row in the profile.

Look at the profile to see that Blocks A and B overlap, thanks to the addition of the constant, which when woven adds width to each of the blocks in different sheds. Sections of the constants appear to be outlined, but the outline threads, the first or last thread of the blocks, actually belong to the blocks. These outline threads are used to separate colors. Each new group of different-colored blocks is outlined with a different color.

PROJECT NOTES

Warp Maysville 8/4 cotton carpet warp in the following colors: red brown #7 (90 yd), bronze #40 (195 yd), dusty rose #19 (225 yd), copper #35 (195 yd), dubonnet #71 (225 yd)
Outline: 8 yd each navy blue #5, forest green #12, duck #47, black #2

Thick Weft Two 1" fabric strips, the front of one strip wound to the back of the other strip on a rag shuttle

Thin Weft Maysville 8/4 cotton carpet warp in a color to match the fabric

Warp Sett 20 ends per inch, 1 thread per heddle

Reed 10 dent, sleyed 2 ends per dent

Width in Reed 12³/₄"

Finished Width Same or slightly wider, measured at the fold of the fabric

Total Ends 256

Number of Placemats Four

Follow the Cloth Length through Warp Length as in the Checkerboard Placemats.

WARP COLOR ORDER

Follow the warp color order from left to right and wind a 3³/₄-yard warp, two threads at a time. After winding the warp, follow the directions for Warping the Loom (page 25).

THREADING

The threads from the lease sticks are in the proper threading sequence. Thread the warp alternately on two shafts directly from the profile draft. Be sure to place the outline threads

	12x	20x	20x	20x	12x	
red brown	I				I	24
navy blue	I				I	2
bronze				I I 18 I I		52
forest green				I I		2
dusty rose			I I 18 I I			60
duck			I I			2
dubonnet		I I 18 I I				60
black		I I				2
copper	I I 18 I I					52
warp color order						256

2	///////...		128
1	///////...		128

threading

on the same shaft adjacent to the block that
they outline.

TIE-UP

Each shaft is tied to a separate treadle. The
first treadle weaves the thick weft—the calico

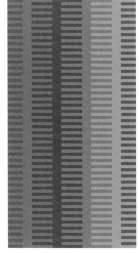

placemat 3 tie-up and treadling order

Vermilion placemat 3

Following the heading, the entire body of the mat is
woven with the thick pick. The block order shifts every
pick for a total of 81 thick picks.

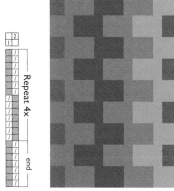

placemat 1 tie-up and treadling order

Vermilion placemat 1

Weave the first block with 7 thick picks before changing
the block with an extra pick of thin weft. The blocks
change nine times for a total of 63 thick picks.

fabric—followed by the second treadle with
the thin weft—carpet warp.

WEAVING

Spread the warp to the width of the reed
by weaving 6–8 picks of 8/4 cotton. Follow
the directions for Weaving an Elastic Heading (page 38) and weave an elongated
heading that will become a triple-folded hem.
There are three different treadling variations—weave each mat differently or design
your own pattern as you weave vs planning
it out ahead. Only two treadles are used to
alternate thick and thin wefts.

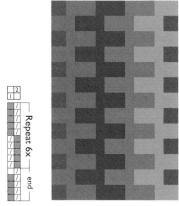

placemat 2 tie-up and treadling order

Vermilion placemat 2

Weave the first block with 5 thick picks before omitting
the thin pick at the block change. The blocks change
thirteen times for a total of 65 thick picks.

FINISHING

Make triple-folded hems, following the directions for Headings and Hems (page 140).

All three placemats, with a range of 63 to 81 thick picks per mat, should measure the same length after shrinkage. Take note of the different methods used as you weave and record measurements accurately for future reference. The techniques you learned in this section and the lessons required to weave them will be repeated as the number of blocks and shafts increases throughout the book. Practice weaving with two blocks until you feel confident about moving ahead to weaving with more than two blocks.

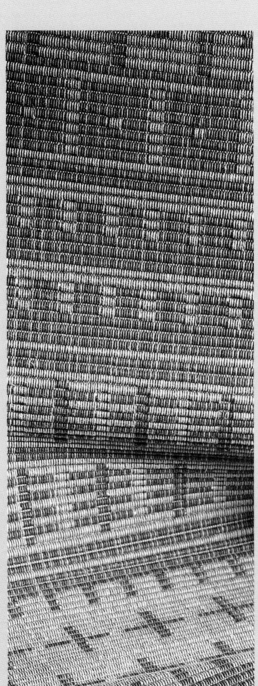

3-Block Designs

our shafts are necessary for threading three blocks because each block is threaded on a pair of adjacent shafts—Block A on shafts 1 and 2, Block B on shafts 3 and 4, Block C on shafts 2 and 1; there is no D block. The threading order, tie-down methods, tie-ups, and weaving blocks expand to four shafts and four treadles.

Refer to the Weaving chapter for information on headings, beating, and changing blocks; directions specific to an individual project or to emphasize a certain point are noted with each project.

3-Block, 4-Shaft Projects

1910 Revisited Rug

More than any other project in the book, this long, narrow, fringed rug captures the essence of a traditional Swedish rep rug. The inspiration comes from a group of rugs woven about 1910, now in the collection of the Swedish Handcraft Society. These dark-colored rugs of browns, dark yellow, orange, blues, and Turkey red, with little contrast between pattern and background, were used in farmhouses where their dark colors wouldn't show the dirt that would inevitably be tracked in.

Two new approaches—a newly expanded color scheme, including the use of constants, and the three-block design—blend with the traditional Swedish style of threading two threads per heddle, four per dent, making it easy to treadle with the doubling of threads in the heddles. The doubled warp ends furthermore cover the weft better than they would using the same thread single in the heddle at 30 ends per inch. However, at this point, consider the choice of your thick fabric weft as the interaction of the warp and weft is important to the overall appearance of the finished product. I integrated the thick weft with the colors of the warp by my choice of fabric. The weft, no matter how visible, should complement the warp, never fight or detract from it.

PROJECT NOTES

Warp Maysville 8/4 cotton carpet warp
Background: linen #46 (2278 yd)
Pattern: rust #67 (714 yd), Kentucky cardinal #23 (204 yd), forest green #12 (408 yd), red brown #7 (102 yd), copper #35 (102 yd), smokey blue #6 (68 yd)

Thick Weft Two 1" strips of fabric, the front of one strip wound to the back of the other strip on a rag shuttle

Thin Weft Maysville 8/4 cotton carpet warp in a color to match the fabric or warp

Warp Sett 40 ends per inch, 2 threads per heddle

Reed 10 dent, sleyed 4 ends per dent

Width in Reed $22\,^3/_4$"

Finished Width Same or slightly wider, measured at the fold of the fabric

Total Ends 912

Cloth Length 85"

Raw Length Woven under tension to $102\,^1/_2$"

Take-Up 17% (during weaving) $14\,^1/_2$"

Shrinkage 17% (after weaving) $14\,^1/_2$"

Tie-On 16" (becomes fringe)

Loom Waste 16" (4" per shaft; becomes fringe)

Total Warp Length 146" or 4 yards

WARP COLOR ORDER

Follow the warp color order and wind a 4-yard warp, two threads at a time. Warp threads are wound in pairs—I suggest loading the spool rack with two tubes of the same color, side by side, for ease during winding. Wind four warp threads at a time—two pattern, two background (one pair each). When winding the constant, both pairs of threads will be the same color.

When changing colors, simply splice the ends of the old and new colors together (see Splicing, page 20) at either end of the board or mill and continue warping. Wind half the warp, stopping after winding six linen, six rust, tie the cross and cinch ties, and remove the warp from the board or mill. Begin the second half of the warp with six linen, six rust, and continue. After winding the warp, follow the directions for Warping the Loom (page 25).

warp color order

		16x	4x	4x	4x	16x	4x	4x	4x	12x	4x	4x	4x	12x	4x	4x	4x	8x	12x	4x	12x	4x	12x	8x	4x	4x	4x	12x	4x	4x	4x	12x	4x	4x	4x	16x	4x	4x	4x	16x	
linen			2		2	2		2	2	2	2		2	2	2	2		2		2	2		2	2		2	2	2	2		2	2	2	2		2	2	2		2	536
rust				2	2		2			2		2			2		2			2		2			2			2			2			2			2 2		2		168
Kentucky cardinal		2 2				2			2				2															2													48
forest green								2				2				2										2				2										96
red brown														2																										24
copper																	2																							24
smokey blue																			2		2																			16
																																									912

threading

	112
4	112
3	116
2	116
1	

THREADING

In the threading profile, note that the colors of Block A change between copper, red brown, and rust. It's not necessary that all repeats of a given block be identical in color. The use of multiple colors makes the design more interesting. Follow the draft and thread two identical threads in every heddle.

Because the warp is very dense, tie it to the front tie-rod in 1" bundles. The 16" of warp allows for tying onto the rod and becomes twisted fringe; the loom waste becomes fringe on the opposite end.

TIE-UP

Treadles are numbered from left to right. Treadle 1 raises shafts 1 and 3, treadle 2 raises shafts 2 and 4, treadle 3 raises shafts 1 and 4, and treadle 4 raises shafts 2 and 3.

WEAVING

Spread the warp to the width of the reed by weaving 6–8 picks of 8/4 cotton, using treadles 1 and 2. Follow the directions for Weaving an Elastic Heading (page 38). Weave the heading with the same pair of adjacent treadles that will weave the first thick pick to ensure a smooth transition from the heading into the rug. Because the warp is dense, the

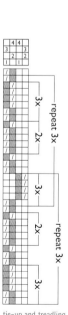

tie-up and treadling

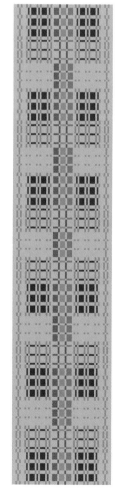

heading may tend to weave wider than the width in reed. To maintain the correct width, check the width in reed every time the beater strikes the web. Weave a 1" heading and leave the shuttle at the selvedge. Weave the thick weft to the left, taper the end, wrap the selvedge, tuck the tail into the same shed, close the shed and beat. Follow with the thin weft in the same direction on the opposite shed of the thick weft, change shed and beat.

Weave the rug following the treadling draft. After weaving the body of the rug; cut off the thick weft, taper the end, wrap the selvedge, and tuck the tail into the same shed. Weave a pick of thin weft and continue to weave a 1" heading using the same pair of treadles. I like to secure the last few wefts to the warp with a small amount of flexible fabric glue. Allow the glue to dry before loosening the tension and cutting the warp at the back tie-rod.

FINISHING

Finish the weaving as soon as possible after removing it from the loom, following the directions for Fringes (page 143). Remnants of the glue will be removed as you remove some of the heading in preparation for making the fringe.

Saguaro Placemats

The largest of the cacti, the great saguaros, dot the desert landscape in southern Arizona in a multitude of formal postures and comical poses. These cacti were the inspiration for these colorful, cheery, whimsical, and fun-to-weave placemats.

The warp contains eighteen colors so the winding takes extra time and attention. Because each thread changes color to create form and dimension, it is necessary to cut and splice every pattern thread in the warp. Use the colors as suggested or substitute your own to complement your dishes and décor.

A three-block design is necessary to enable you to use a single block for the main trunk of the cactus. Combined blocks make the arms of the cactus in different arrangements and configurations. Shading from light to dark in the warp gives the main body and arms of the cactus a feeling of roundness. Two alternating colors are used to make the extensions between the arms and body of the cactus. Seven constants run the length of the design, four of which are used on either side of outlined borders. Constants also separate the cacti. The single block between the cacti represents the sun or moon.

PROJECT NOTES

Warp Maysville 8/4 cotton carpet warp
Background and Constants: Spanish blue #72 (928 yd)
Border: duck #47 (8 yd), aqua #45 (40 yd), velvet #84 (8 yd), dubonnet #71 (20 yd)
Saguaro 1: burnt orange #18 (12 yd), copper #35 (12 yd), poppy #41 (36 yd), red #22 (36 yd), cardinal #23 (12 yd), cranberry #38 (12 yd)
Saguaro 2: burnt orange #18 (12 yd), coral #32 (12 yd), dusty rose #19 (28 yd), dubonnet #71 (28 yd), red brown #7 (12 yd), velvet #84 (12 yd)
Saguaro 3: gold #10 (12 yd), bronze #40 (12 yd), dusty rose #19 (52 yd), copper #35 (52 yd), rust #67 (12 yd), dark brown #8 (12 yd)
Moon or Sun: ecru #28 (12 yd), tan #30 (12 yd)

Thick Weft Two 1" strips of calico fabric, the front of one strip wound to the back of the other strip on a rag shuttle

Thin Weft Maysville 8/4 cotton carpet warp in a color to match the fabric or warp

Warp Sett 30 ends per inch, 1 thread per heddle

Reed 15 dent, sleyed 2 ends per dent

Width in Reed 12$\frac{1}{3}$"

Finished Width Same or slightly wider, measured at the fold of the fabric

Total Ends 370

Number of Placemats Four

Cloth Length Four placemats each finished to 18$\frac{1}{2}$" = 74"

Raw Length Each placemat woven under tension to 22"

Take-Up 17% (during weaving) 12$\frac{1}{2}$"

Shrinkage 17% (after weaving) 12$\frac{1}{2}$"

Tie-On 10"

Hems 1$\frac{3}{4}$" × 8 edges = 14"

Loom Waste 16" (4" per shaft)

Total Warp Length 139" or 4 yards

WARP COLOR ORDER

Follow the warp color order and wind a 4-yard warp, two threads at a time. The constants and background threads throughout are Spanish blue. It will be easier to wind the warp if you first load the spool rack with the colors used in the border first. After winding the border, load the spool rack with the colors of Saguaro 1. After winding Saguaro 1 reload the spool rack for Saguaro 2, followed by the moon/sun and then Saguaro 3.

warp color order

left border

	5x	5x	5x	
Spanish blue	16			16	51
duck					2
aqua					10
velvet					2
dubonnet					5
					70

saguaro 1

	5x	2x	2x	4x	
Spanish blue					10	48
gold						3
bronze						3
dusty rose						13
copper						13
rust						3
dark brown						3
						86

saguaro 2

	2x	2x	
Spanish blue			26
orange			3
coral			3
dusty rose			7
dubonnet			7
red brown			3
velvet			3
			52

	3x	
Spanish blue	10	10	26
ecru			3
tan			3
			32

saguaro 3

	2x	4x	
Spanish blue			30
burnt orange			3
copper			3
poppy red			9
red			9
Kentucky cardinal			3
cranberry			3
			60

right border

	5x	5x	5x	
Spanish blue	16			16	51
duck					2
aqua					10
velvet					2
dubonnet					5
					70

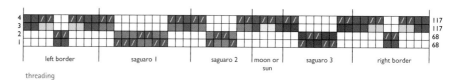

		117
4		117
3		117
2		68
1		68

left border   saguaro 1   saguaro 2   moon or sun   saguaro 3   right border

threading

Repeat the border. After winding the warp, follow the directions for Warping the Loom (page 25).

TIE-UP

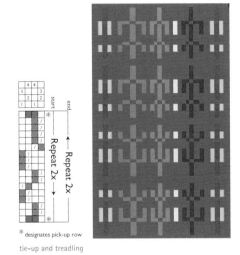

* designates pick-up row

tie-up and treadling

WEAVING

Spread the warp to the width of the reed by weaving 6–8 picks of 8/4 cotton, using the same pair of treadles that will weave the first thick pick. Follow the directions for Weaving an Elastic Heading (page 38). Continue weaving, following the treadling draft. In this 3-block, 4-shaft tie-up, no shed raises all of the background threads to weave the separation rows between the cacti. Therefore, it's necessary to pick up the background threads on a pick-up stick. This is easier than it sounds. Choose the treadle that raises most of the background threads. Step on that treadle and insert a pick-up stick into the shed under the background threads until reaching pattern threads. At the point where the pattern threads begin, change to the other treadle of the pair to bring up the background and include it on the stick. Continue to alternate raising background and pattern until you have picked up all of the background threads. Turn the stick on its side to create a shed and weave the thick weft; remove the sword and beat. Follow the same procedure, beginning on the opposite treadle, and pick up all of the pattern threads. Turn the stick on its side and weave the thin (tie-down) weft. After weaving the separating rows, revert to the treadling order and continue. The varying heights and configurations of the saguaros are accomplished in the treadling.

FINISHING

Make triple-folded hems, following the directions for Headings and Hems (page 140).

Circle of Life Sash

This sash is reminiscent of the belts woven by Hopi men and Navajo women and are still used ceremonially, worn by members of both genders. Such sashes were used to cinch a woman's dress and also reportedly tied to a pole or tree and pulled on by a woman when giving birth, then afterward tied around the waist to keep her abdomen firm. A similar sash is worn by the Hopi kachinas during the dances and ceremonies on the mesas. I was inspired not only by the pleasing appearance of these tribal sashes but also by the manner in which they are wrapped and tied for wearing, in this case, Navajo fashion.

The fine weft threads make this long linen sash delicate and soft; a twisted fringe makes it even longer. One fringed end of the sash is left free to hang while the remainder of the belt encircles the body and overlaps the layer beneath. The other fringed end of the wrapped belt is held while the uppermost fringe is fed down behind the layer underneath and brought out at the bottom. Then the lower fringe is fed underneath to the top of the sash. Tie each of these twisted fringes in a bow or slipknot to the next closest strand. It appears to be casually tied at the waist but is actually held quite securely.

This sash is woven with natural 20/3 in a 3-block design. A central constant stripe runs the length of the sash as do narrow constant stripes that bisect each of the single and combined blocks within the pattern. The design blocks build from the center stripe to form rows of shallow chevrons that form a stepped circle when inverted. The selvedge edge is also a constant divided by alternating color strips.

PROJECT NOTES

Warp 20/3 natural linen (260 yd), 16/2 linen: blue (205 yd), red (40 yd), wine (30 yd), green (30 yd)

Thick Weft Four strands of 8/3 linen, wound together

Thin Weft One strand of 20/3 linen

Warp Sett 50 ends per inch, 1 thread per heddle

Reed 10 dent, sleyed 5 ends per dent

Width in Reed $4^1/_2$" (11.5 cm)

Finished Width Same or slightly wider, measured at the fold of the weft

Total Ends 226

Cloth Length 48"

Raw Length Woven under tension to 58"

Take-Up 10% (during weaving) $4^1/_5$"

Shrinkage 10% (after weaving) $4^1/_5$"

Tie-On 15" (becomes fringe)

Loom Waste 16" (4" per shaft; becomes fringe)

Total Warp Length 89" or $2^1/_2$ yards

WARP COLOR ORDER

Follow the warp color order and wind a $2^1/_2$-yard warp, two threads at a time. After winding the warp, follow the directions for Warping the Loom (page 25).

					4x		8x		8x		4x				4x		8x		8x		4x						
natural	12	2	2	12	1		1		1		1				1		1		1		1		12	2	2	12	104
blue		2	2	2		1		1		1		10	2	10		1		1		1		1		2	2	2	82
red					2		2		2			2		2		2				2							16
wine					2			2		2		2			2			2		2							12
green						2		2		2			2		2		2		2								12
																										226

warp color order

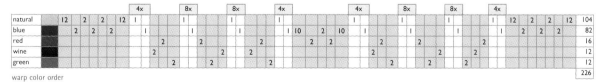

threading

4																							81
3																							81
2																							32
1																							32

THREADING

Thread this 3-block pattern on four shafts; there is no D block. Thread the constants on shafts 3 and 4. The constants and Block B share the same pair of adjacent shafts.

WEAVING

Tie on, leaving a 15" length of warp for fringe. Weave a 1" heading with the natural 20/3 linen before you begin the thick weft. Some of the excess heading will be cut away during finishing. Leave the shuttle attached at the right side of the web. Change shed, and begin the thick weft at the right side.

TIE-UP

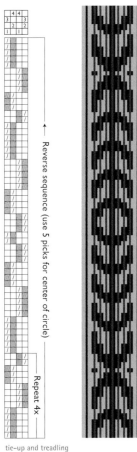

tie-up and treadling

Tuck the tails at least 1" into the same shed and splay each end of the weft so that they don't all overlap in the same spot. Follow the treadling draft. Linen is similar to wire in that it doesn't shrink or stretch; pull the weft straight across the shed and beat firmly. Turn the strands of linen weft neatly at the selvedges.

When the body of the sash has been woven, relax the tension on the cloth beam and cut the warp along the back tie-rod. From the front of the loom, pull the loom waste gently through the heddles and reed and untie the warp from the front tie-rod.

FINISHING

Cover the sash with a damp cloth and press with an iron set on "steam." Because the weaving is delicate and fine, retain 8–9 picks of 20/3 linen in the heading. Remove the excess heading in 1" sections as you tie the fringe. Follow the directions for Fringes (page 143), twisting the two strands of the same color 16/2 dyed linen together and securing the twisted strands with a nearly invisible half hitch. There is no need to twist the natural 20/3 linen because the dense sett keeps the fine weft from unweaving.

3-Block, 8-Shaft Projects

There are advantages to threading fewer blocks on more shafts, especially when the number of shafts is twice the number of blocks. Three-block designs threaded on eight shafts allow each design block to be threaded on a separate pair of shafts, leaving the extra pair of shafts for the constants. In this way, the pattern or background of each block can be used singly or combined in several arrangements. Spreading a dense warp over more shafts also creates a better shed.

Homage to the Long Walk Placemats

Navajo chief-style blankets are probably the most recognizable textiles of the Classic Period. Woven wider than long, these blankets evolved over the course of the nineteenth century. There are general characteristics to these blankets, but all have variations. Those of the first phase, circa 1800–1860, were woven with simple, broad horizontal stripes in blue, brown, and white. In blankets of the second phase, 1860–1875, the color red is added along with the blue, brown and white horizontal stripes and the stripes are interrupted by elongated rectangles. Third-phase blankets 1870–1890 are distinguished by quarter, half, and whole diamonds in red, blue, and brown placed against broad stripes of black, blue, and white. These premier works of art seemed to give way near the end of the century when Navajo life and textiles were changed forever. Tired of skirmishes with the Navajo, the United States government rounded up members of the Navajo tribe and marched them to Fort Sumner, New Mexico, near Bosque Redondo and imprisoned them during the period 1863–1868. Men, women, and children were forced to walk the entire distance and many perished along the way. Hence, the naming of this piece, Homage to the Long Walk.

Navajo weaving is plentiful in the Flagstaff area and has undoubtedly influenced my own sense of design, composition, and color. I saw many beautiful chief blankets at the Museum of Northern Arizona in 1986 when, as a volunteer, I assisted in inventorying of the entire Navajo textile collection. The second-phase blankets especially intrigued me. The aniline red yarns and the raveled cochineal-dyed wools were faded and mellow. The natural color of the handspun wool had yellowed, and the natural brown-black and dyed indigo blue handspun wools were mottled.

The realization that I could admire the blankets only from afar led me to design and weave a rendition of my own. I wanted my rug to emulate an old faded chief blanket, and the idea of using Navajo symbolism in multiples of four—the four directions and the four sacred mountains—made designing more exciting. The design elements consist of units of four large squares made up of every shade of red and related colors I could find to resemble the faded reds in the second-phase blankets. The red squares are bordered toward the inside by vertical blue rectangles positioned next to a continuous brown stripe. Smaller blue rectangles and brown spots pulsate along the outside edge. At 32" wide, set at 30 ends per inch, this rug was a huge endeavor. The warp alone contains 960 ends, 12 1/2 yards long, and weighs 7 1/2 pounds. That translates to 12,000 yards of warp. I wove two samples, each 1 yard long, and made minor changes in the threading before I wove the 21' runner. The finished rug weighs 11 1/2 pounds and measures 32" × 17' 8". I bound both ends with leather using a leather punch and sewing through the layers. I sliced the ends of the leather for fringe and added tin jinglers.

Not every weaver wants or needs to fulfill such a dream as weaving an interpretation of a second-phase Navajo chief blanket, so even though my rug is pictured here, I've scaled it down to placemat size for this project. It's the same threading; the treadling is abbreviated from the rug.

PROJECT NOTES

Warp Maysville 8/4 cotton carpet warp in a range of naturals (792 yd), browns (72 yd), blues (180 yd), and reds (360 yd). Mix and blend the colors as you wind the warp or substitute other colors using the draft as a guide.

Thick Weft Two 1" strips of fabric, the front of one strip wound to the back of the other strip on a rag shuttle

Thin Weft Maysville 8/4 cotton carpet warp in a color to match the fabric

Warp Sett 24 ends per inch, 1 thread per heddle

Reed 12 dent, sleyed 2 ends per dent

Width in Reed 13"

Finished Width Same or slightly wider, measured at the fold of the fabric

Total Ends 312

Number of Placemats Four

Cloth Length Four placemats each finished to $18\frac{1}{2}$" = 74"

Raw Length Each placemat woven under tension to 22"

Take-Up 17% (during weaving) $12\frac{2}{3}$"

Shrinkage 17% (after weaving) $12\frac{2}{3}$"

Tie-On 10"

Hems $1\frac{3}{4}$" × 8 edges = 14"

Loom Waste 32" (4" per shaft)

Total Warp Length 155" or $4\frac{1}{2}$ yards

WARP COLOR ORDER

Follow the warp color order and wind a $4\frac{1}{2}$-yard warp, two threads at a time. After winding the warp, follow the directions for Warping the Loom (page 25).

THREADING

Thread pattern then ground throughout the blocks.

naturals		8	4	8	40	8	12	8		8	12	8	40	8	4	8	176
browns			4					8							4		16
blue range				8			12				12			8			40
red range					40								40				80

warp color order — 312

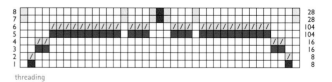

threading

TIE-UP

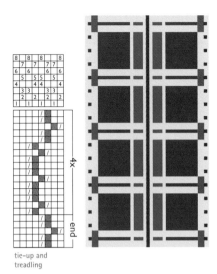

tie-up and
treadling

WEAVING

Spread the warp to the width of the reed by weaving 6–8 picks of 8/4 cotton, using the same pair of treadles that will weave the first thick pick. Follow the directions for Weaving an Elastic Heading (page 38). Continue weaving, following the treadling draft. The C blocks are two different colors, but each of the other blocks could be of different colors as well. Experiment to create your own colorway.

FINISHING

Make triple-folded hems, following the directions for Headings and Hems (page 140).

Hohokam Runner and Placemats

Living in the Southwest provides me with an enormous source of inspiration as well as a vivid and extensive color palette. *The Hohokam: Desert Farmers and Craftsmen*, a study by Emil W. Haury of the ancient people who built Snaketown, Pueblo Grande, Casa Grande, and Montezuma Castle, inspired the name of this project. The Pima, Maricopa, and Papago peoples are believed to have descended from the Hohokam (whose name means "all used up" in Pima), who migrated from Mexico into the Valley of the Sun and north as far as Sedona and Flagstaff.

Red-on-buff pottery produced by the Hohokam during the Gila Butte Phase (A.D. 550–700), specifically, a tiny potsherd with painted vertical lines and cross bars in rows that shifted in alignment, influenced these textiles. I wound a warp, threaded a simple 3-block pattern A-B-C-B-A on eight shafts, allowing each block to occupy a separate pair of adjacent shafts. The treadles were tied up to allow the use of any single block, any two, or all three. As I began to weave the runner, I discovered that by combining sheds, I could weave crosses with solid or open centers, boxes that were positive or negative, empty or occupied by a small square in the center, shifting vertical bars with cross bars, solid lines, or lines with jagged teeth closely set or spread apart. The design possibilities were amazing, my original expectations so simple. In your own designing, look carefully to take advantage of every shed's potential to create untapped design possibilities.

I have presented the runner and place-mats as separate projects as I prefer to wind two separate warps. A single, long combined warp is possible, but tension problems can waste valuable time and energy. If you do wind a combined warp, I advise you to cut off the runner after weaving and then retie the warp for the placemats. Be sure to allow an extra tie-on length for the second project.

Hohokam Runner

PROJECT NOTES

Warp Maysville 8/4 cotton carpet warp in two color groupings:
Background: linen #46 (606 yd)
Pattern: Mix of rust #67, red brown #7, and brown #8 (662 yd total)

Thick Weft Two 1" strips of fabric, the front of one strip wound to the back of the other strip on a rag shuttle

Thin Weft Maysville 8/4 cotton carpet warp in a color to match the fabric

Warp Sett 30 ends per inch, 1 thread per heddle

Reed 15 dent, sleyed 2 ends per dent

Width in Reed 12"

Finished Width Same or slightly wider, measured at the fold of the fabric

Total Ends 362

Cloth Length 64"

Raw Length Woven under tension to 77"

Take-Up 17% (during weaving) 11"

Shrinkage 17% (after weaving) 11"

Tie-On 8"

Loom Waste 32" (4" per shaft; becomes fringe)

Total Warp Length 126" or 3¹/₂ yards

mix: browns/rust				8		8	5	12	5	12	5	12	5	12	5	12	5	12	5	12	5	12	5	12	4	8		8	189
linen						8		5	12	5	12	5	12	5	12	5	12	5	12	5	12	5	12	5	12	4		8		173
warp color order																														362

threading

TIE-UP

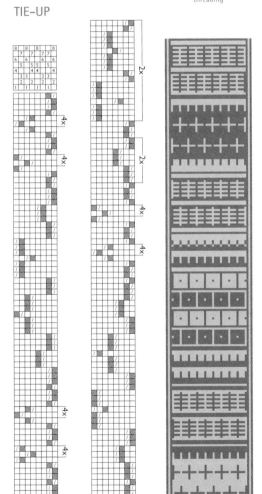

tie-up and
treadling

WARP COLOR ORDER

Follow the warp color order and wind a
3¹/₂-yard warp. Wind the 8-end constant,
mixing the three colors for variety. Continue
with 8 ends of linen, and then 8 mixed. Then
wind the block colors, combining 3 ends of
the linen and 3 ends of the color mix. Repeat
the constants to balance the other edge. After
winding the warp, follow the directions for
Warping the Loom (page 25).

THREADING

Constant stripes form the borders along the
selvedges. Thread the constants on shafts 7
and 8; thread the blocks as usual, keeping the
linen as background and mixing the browns
as you like.

WEAVING

Spread the warp to the width of the reed by
weaving 4–6 picks of 8/4 cotton. Follow the
directions for Weaving an Elastic Heading
(page 38). Weave the runner following the
treadling draft. Weave to the end, cut off the
thick weft, and tuck the tail into the same
shed. Weave the final heading, using the same
pair of treadles used for the last thick pick.

Loosen the tension on the warp and cut along the back tie-rod.

FINISHING

Follow the directions for Fringes (page 143).

Hohokam Placemats

PROJECT NOTES

Warp Maysville 8/4 cotton carpet warp in two color groupings:

Background: linen #46 (4545 yd)

Pattern: rust #67, red brown #7, and brown #8 (4965 yd total)

Wefts through Total Ends Follow as per Runner

Number of Placemats Eight

Cloth Length Each placemat finished to 18¹⁄₄" = 146"

Raw Length Each placemat woven under tension to 22"

Take-Up 17% (during weaving) 25"

Shrinkage 17% (after weaving) 25"

Hems 1³⁄₄" × 16 edges = 28"

Tie-On 10"

Loom Waste 32" (4" per shaft)

Total Warp Length 266" or 7¹⁄₂ yards

WARP COLOR ORDER

Follow the warp color order and wind a 7¹⁄₂-yard warp. Follow the directions for the Runner. After winding the warp, follow the directions for Warping the Loom (page 25).

THREADING

Follow the directions for the Runner.

TIE-UP

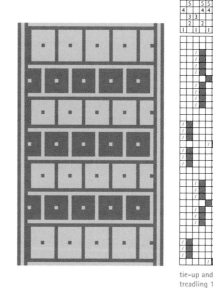

tie-up and treadling 1

WEAVING

Spread the warp to the width of the reed by weaving 6–8 picks of 8/4 cotton, using the same pair of treadles that will weave the first thick pick. Follow the directions for Weaving an Elastic Heading (page 38). Weave two of each of the three placemat designs. Weave two more of your own design or repeat one of your favorites. The designs show the dramatic effects of changing the treadling order. After each placemat, weave a 1³⁄₄" heading, using the same pair of treadles used to weave the last thick weft. To separate the mats, weave two picks of a brightly colored strand of 8/4 cotton. Begin a new heading and continue with another placemat. After weaving the last placemat, loosen the tension on the warp and cut at the back tie-rod.

tie-up and
treadling 2

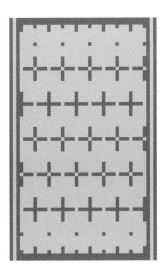

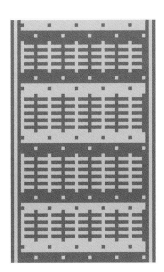

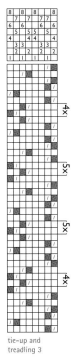

tie-up and
treadling 3

FINISHING

Follow the directions for a triple-folded hem in Headings and Hems (page 140). On the mats with the same treadling, flip one of them over and hem it so the "back" side is facing up. You'll then have eight unique, coordinated placemats.

Saguaro Cactus Runner

The giant saguaro cactus, the state flower of Arizona, has a tall, thick, columnar stem 18"–24" inches in diameter. It grows very slowly, about 1" a year, but to a height of 15'–50'. Some have several large arms that curve upward; others stand without arms. At dawn with a lingering moon or at dusk with a setting sun, these magnificent cacti appear magical and whimsical against the desert sky and take on dramatic color schemes that turn them shades of pastel and amber. I hoped to capture the essence of the moment in this long table runner displaying saguaro cacti in different colors and sizes.

This project illustrates how threading a 3-block design on eight shafts allows more freedom in combining blocks in the weaving than you would have with four shafts because each block is threaded on a separate pair of shafts. Compare it with the 3-block Saguaro placemats (page 74), which were woven on four shafts. A picked-up shed was necessary because two blocks shared the same pair of shafts, and it was otherwise impossible to combine all of the background blocks needed to weave and separate the horizontal rows of cactus. When a similar design is threaded on eight shafts, the background of each block is combined in the tie-up to create the separating row. The cactus configurations are also woven differently. The trunk of each cactus in the runner is solid without the unavoidable open space of the cacti in the placemats. Although the weaving technique remains the same aside from the pick-up, the wider variety of block combinations makes the design more interesting.

PROJECT NOTES

Warp Maysville 8/4 cotton carpet warp in the following colors:

Background and Constants: rust #67 (1528 yd)
Pattern:
Left Border: red brown #7 (16 yd), royal blue #4 (48 yd), dusty rose #19 (24 yd)
Cactus 1: purple #25 (12 yd), cranberry #38 (12 yd), dubonnet #71 (12 yd), copper #35 (60 yd), old rose #20 (12 yd), coral #32 (60 yd), dusty rose #19 (12 yd), peach #11 (12 yd)

Cactus 2: forest green #12 (8 yd), kelly green #73 (88 yd), duck #47 (12 yd), sage #33 (12 yd), aqua green #45 (8 yd), colonial green #14 (8 yd), myrtle green #15 (8 yd), purple #25 (4 yd), light blue #75 (4 yd), colonial blue #3 (8 yd)
Sun: red #22 (4 yd), poppy #41 (12 yd), coral #32 (12 yd), cranberry #38 (4 yd)
Cactus 3: black #2 (4 yd), purple #25 (12 yd), navy blue #5 (8 yd), smokey blue #6 (60 yd), slate gray #13 (8 yd), Spanish blue #4 (80 yd), colonial blue #3 (12 yd), lavender #21 (4 yd), forest green #12 (4 yd)
Right Border: dubonnet #71 (8 yd), dusty rose # 19 (40 yd), coral #32 (12 yd), dark brown #8 (8 yd), duck #47 (24 yd)

Thick Weft Two 1" strips of fabric, the front of one strip wound to the back of the other strip on a rag shuttle

Thin Weft Maysville 8/4 cotton carpet warp in a color to match the fabric or warp

Warp Sett 30 ends per inch, 1 thread per heddle

Reed 15 dent, sleyed 2 ends per dent

Width in reed 18 ³/₄"

Finished Width Same or slightly wider, measured at the fold of the fabric

Total Ends 560

Cloth Length 90 ¹/₂"

Raw Length Woven under tension to 109"

Take-Up 17% (during weaving) 15 ²/₅"

Shrinkage 17% (after weaving) 15 ²/₅"

Tie-On 10" (becomes hem)

Loom Waste 32" (4" per shaft)

Total Warp Length 147" or 4 yards

WARP COLOR ORDER

Follow the warp color order and wind a 4-yard warp. Warp threads are wound in pairs—I suggest loading the spool rack with one tube of the background and one tube of pattern, side by side, for ease during winding. Each cactus has a different color arrangement. The threads on the cacti begin with the darkest color and gradually become lighter to give the impression of a third dimension. This requires that each pattern thread of the cactus trunk and arms, eight threads each, be spliced (see Splicing, page 20) when changing colors. Two colors alternate to make the arm extensions. After winding the warp, follow the directions for Warping the Loom (page 25).

THREADING

The threading follows the warp color order, beginning with the Right border, Cactus 3, Sun, Cactus 2, Cactus 1, and ending with the left border.

warp color order

left border

										Total
rust	16	1	6	1	6	1	6	1	16	54
red brown	1	1	1	1						4
royal blue			6			6				12
dusty rose					6					6
										76

cactus 1 (reds)

		Total
rust	1 1 1 1 1 1 1 12 1 1 1 1 1 1 1 1 12 1 1 1 1 1 24	72
purple	1 1 1	3
new cranberry	1 1 1	3
dubonnet	1 1 1	3
copper	1 6 1 6 1	15
old rose	1 1 1	3
coral	1 6 1 6 1	15
dusty rose	1 1 1	3
peach	1 1 1	3
		120

cactus 2 (greens)

		Total
rust	1 1 1 1 1 2 1 8 1 1 1 1 2 1 1 8 1 1 1 2 1 1	40
forest green	1	2
kelly green	1 1 1	3
duck	1 1 1	3
kelly green	1 1 8 8 2 1	19
sage	2 1	3
aqua green	1 1	2
colonial green	1 1	2
myrtle green	1 1	2
purple	1	1
light blue	1 1	2
colonial blue	2	2
		80

sun

		Total
rust	52 1 1 1 1 1 1 1 1 52	112
red	1	
poppy	1 1 1	3
coral	1 1 1	3
new cranberry	1	1
		120

cactus 3 (blues)

		Total
rust	1 1 1 1 1 2 1 12 1 1 1 1 1 1 1 12 1 1 4 2	48
black	1	1
purple	1 1 1	3
navy blue	1 1	2
smokey blue	1 6 6 1	15
slate gray	1 1	2
Spanish blue	2 6 1 1 6 4	20
colonial blue	1 2	3
lavender	1	1
forest green	1	1
		96

right border

		Total
rust	16 1 1 2 1 3 1 6 1 2 1 3 1 1 16	56
dubonnet	1 1	2
dusty rose	2 3 2 3	10
coral	1 1 1 1	4
dark brown	1 1	2
duck	6	6
		80

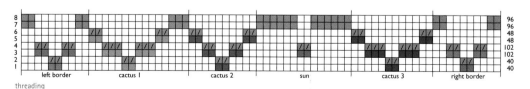

threading

TIE-UP

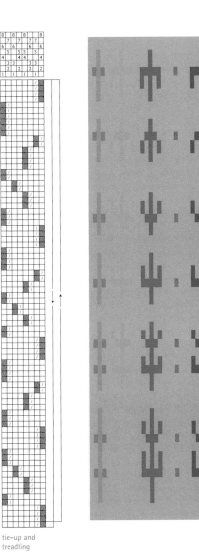

tie-up and
treadling

WEAVING

Spread the warp to the width of the reed by weaving 6–8 picks of 8/4 cotton. Following the directions for Weaving an Elastic Heading (page 38), weave a $1^{3}/_{4}$" heading with the same pair of treadles that will weave the first thick pick. Follow the treadling draft or devise a set of cacti of your own. Reverse the order of treadling at the center of the runner if you would like to weave the remainder of the pattern in reverse.

FINISHING

Follow the directions for Headings and Hems (page 140).

Kayenta Runner and Placemats

Kayenta black-on-white is the term used to identify and describe a type of pre-historic Indian pottery found in northern Arizona. The design elements, painted in black, are so close together and so dense that little of the white background shows, giving the impression of a white design on a black background. These designs were painted on bowls, ladles, and ollas—widemouthed earthenware pots or jars. Small bowls in the collections of the Museum of Northern Arizona inspired this runner and placemats.

I have written two separate Project Notes—one for the runner and one for the placemats. However, since the projects are the same width, you can combine the two warp lengths, saving both warp and time. Allow for each project's cloth lengths, take-up, and shrinkage but only one tie-on, one loom waste, and one fringe between the runner and first placemat, as well as the hems for the placemats. Before combining warp lengths, consider whether your loom has the capacity to hold an 8 ½-yard-long warp. Recheck your calculations before winding.

If you like, you can use a different treadling plan for each project. In fact, you can make each placemat unique by weaving some squares solid and varying which squares have a central dot. Or design something completely different. Record the new designs in your notebook.

Runner

PROJECT NOTES

Warp Maysville 8/4 cotton carpet warp in two color groups:
Background: ecru #28, tan #30, and ivory #58 (483 yd total)
Pattern: black #2 (493 yd total)

Thick Weft Two 1" strips of fabric, the front of one strip wound to the back of the other strip on a rag shuttle

Thin Weft Maysville 8/4 cotton carpet warp in a color to match the fabric

Warp Sett 30 ends per inch, 1 thread per heddle

Reed 15 dent, sleyed 2 ends per dent

Width in Reed 13"

Finished Width Same or slightly wider, measured at the fold of the fabric

Total Ends 390

Cloth Length 30"

Raw Length Woven under tension to 36"

Take-Up 17% (during weaving) 5"

Shrinkage 17% (after weaving) 5"

Tie-On 14" (becomes fringe)

Loom Waste 32" (4" per shaft; becomes fringe)

Total Warp Length 86" or 2 ½ yards

WARP COLOR ORDER

Follow the warp color order and wind a 2 ½-yard warp, two threads at a time. You can intermix the blacks and beiges when winding.

blacks	■	28		12		12	6	3	6		9	3	9		6	3	6		9	3	9		9	3	9		12		12		28	197
beiges			20		12		6	6	3	6	6	9	3	9	6	6	3	6	6	9	3	9	6	9	3	9	6		12		20	193
																															390

warp color order

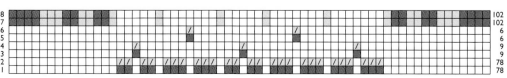

threading

After winding the warp, follow the directions for Warping the Loom (page 25).

THREADING

The constants are on shafts 7 and 8. Intermix the blacks and beiges in threading pattern and background blocks.

WEAVING

Spread the warp to the width of the reed by weaving 6–8 picks of 8/4 cotton. Follow the directions for Weaving an Elastic Heading (page 38). Continue weaving, following the treadling draft.

FINISHING

Follow the directions for Fringes (page 143).

TIE-UP

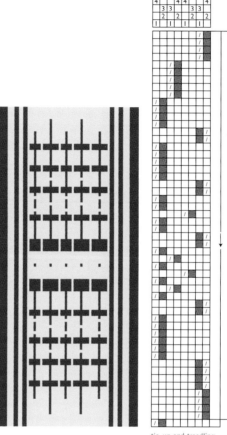

tie-up and treadling

Placemats

(page 38). Continue weaving, following the treadling draft.

PROJECT NOTES

Warp Maysville 8/4 cotton carpet warp in two color groups:

Background: ecru #28, tan #30, ivory #58, natural (BP) (1158 yd total)

Pattern: black #2, jet black (BP), and black direct (CC) (1182 yd total)

Wefts through Total Ends Follow as per Runner

Number of Placemats Six

Cloth Length Each placemat finished to $18^{1}/_{4}" = 109^{1}/_{2}"$

Raw Length Each placemat woven under tension to 22"

Take-Up 17% (during weaving) $18^{3}/_{5}"$

Shrinkage 17% (after weaving) $18^{3}/_{5}"$

Tie-On 10"

Hems $1^{3}/_{4}" \times 12$ edges = 21"

Loom Waste 32" (4" per shaft)

Total Warp Length 210" or 6 yards

WARP COLOR ORDER

As per Runner, but wind a 6-yard warp.

THREADING

As per Runner.

WEAVING

Spread the warp to the width of the reed by weaving 6–8 picks of 8/4 cotton. Follow the directions for Weaving an Elastic Heading

FINISHING

Make triple-folded hems, following the directions for Headings and Hems (page 140).

TIE-UP

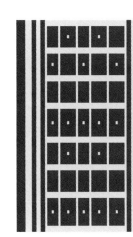

tie-up and treadling

River Runnin' the San Juan Runner

A weaving class at the Museum of Northern Arizona in conjunction with the exhibition Arizona Highways: Celebrating the Tradition offered students an opportunity to use the exhibition as inspiration to record and commemorate the beauty of the southwestern landscapes in a weaving. I chose a photograph of a "gooseneck" along the San Juan River at sunset. A vibrant sunset above the carved, stepped, canyon walls and green vegetation along the sparkling river below contributed to the design and choice of palette.

PROJECT NOTES

Warp Maysville 8/4 cotton carpet warp in two color groups:

Background Mix of blues: royal blue #4, navy blue #5, smokey blue #6, dark navy blue #82 (864 yd total)

Pattern:

Large Squares

Mix 1: copper #35, dubonnet #71, poppy #41, dusty rose #19, burnt orange #18, coral #32 (112 yd total)

Mix 2: rust #67, red brown #7, dark brown #8, copper #35 (112 yd total)

Mix 3: parakeet #48, sage #33, myrtle green #15, duck #47 (96 yd total)

Small Squares

Mix 4: velvet #84, purple #25, dark brown #8 (24 yd total)

Mix 5: duck #47, aqua green #45, turquoise #34 (24 yd total)

Mix 6: dubonnet #71, purple #25, velvet #84 (24 yd total)

Mix 7: copper #35, burnt orange #18, poppy #41 (24 yd total)

Thick Weft Two 1" strips of fabric, the front of one strip wound to the back of the other strip on a rag shuttle

Thin Weft Maysville 8/4 cotton carpet warp in a color to match the fabric

Warp Sett 24 ends per inch, 1 thread per heddle

Reed 12 dent, sleyed 2 ends per dent

Width in Reed 13$^{1}/_{4}$"

Finished Width Same or slightly wider, measured at the fold of the fabric

Total Ends 320

Cloth Length 68"

Raw Length Woven under tension to 82"

Take-Up 17% (during weaving) 11$^{3}/_{5}$"

Shrinkage 17% (after weaving) 11$^{3}/_{5}$"

Headings (1" each end) 2"

Tie-On 14" (becomes fringe)

Loom Waste 32" (4" per shaft; becomes fringe)

Total Warp Length 139" or 4 yards

WARP COLOR ORDER

Follow the warp color order and wind a 4-yard warp. Begin winding with four background threads at a time, cut and splice (see Splicing, page 20) to change the distribution of colors and change the number of threads in your hand as you wind according to the color

blues mix	20	4	18	6	6	24	6	6	6	24	6	6	6	24	6	6	18	4	20	216
copper		4																4		8
mix #4				6																6
mix #1						24														24
mix #5								6												6
mix #2										24										24
mix #6												6								6
mix #3														24						24
mix #7																6				6
																				320

warp color order

groupings. The medium squares contain six pattern and six background threads—wind three pattern and three background threads in your hand at a time. A constant is next; cut off the three pattern threads and wind six background threads. The large squares contain twenty-four pattern threads and twenty-four background threads. If you're comfortable doing so, you can hold four pattern and four background threads. If, however, holding eight threads makes you uneasy, wind with two pattern and two background threads but cut off and change colors every bout to get variety. Follow the warp order but blend both background and pattern colors at random as you wind to offer your own interpretation: it is the way you blend and adapt the use of color that gives a weaving its individuality. After winding the warp, follow the directions for Warping the Loom (page 25).

Tie on to the front tie-rod, leaving 14" to become fringe when the weaving is complete. The loom waste will become the fringe on the opposite end of the weaving.

THREADING

Pattern and background threads will be mixed colors as you thread the blocks. As the blue mix is always your background color, it will be easy to keep track of your block changes.

TIE-UP

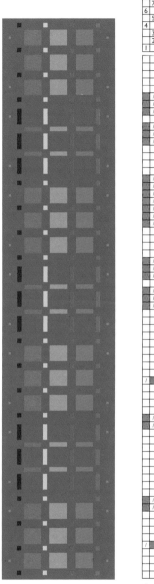

tie-up and treadling

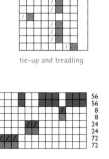

threading

WEAVING

Spread the warp to the width of the reed by weaving 6–8 picks of 8/4 cotton carpet warp. Following the directions for Weaving an Elastic Heading (page 38), weave a 1" heading, using the same pair of treadles that weave the first thick pick. Follow the treadling draft or design your own, recording your design for future reference. When the body of the runner is complete, cut off the thick weft, taper the end, wrap the selvedge, and tuck the tail into the last shed. Weave the final heading with the thin weft, relax the tension on the warp, and cut along the back tie-rod.

FINISHING

Follow the directions for Headings (page 140) and Fringes (page 143). Retain $^1/_4$"–$^5/_8$" of neatly woven and firmly beaten heading as a solid edge against which to tie knots or fringe. I added cones to the ends of my fringe (see Cones or Beads, page 147).

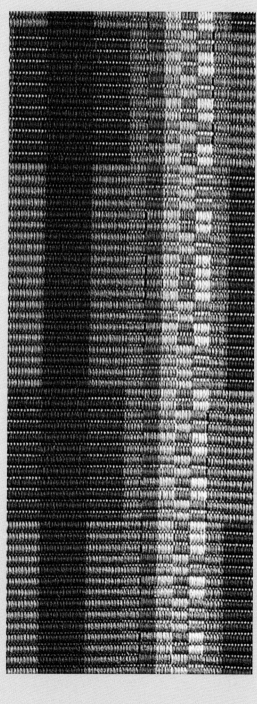

4-Block Designs

      4-block design threaded on four shafts requires that the pattern of Block A to be threaded on shaft 1, background on shaft 2. Thread the pattern of Block B on shaft 3, background on shaft 4. It becomes necessary to thread the C block in the opposite order of Block A and the D block opposite Block B. Transitions between blocks must be smooth. For instance, when a C block follows an A block, two pattern or background threads will lie adjacent to each other. If threaded side by side on the same shaft, even if they are different colors, two threads will always rise or sink together, creating a straight line throughout the weaving. To prevent this, reverse the order of the pattern and background threads of any two blocks that share the same pair of adjacent shafts and continue to alternate shafts.

      Faulty lines, characteristic of rep weave and unavoidable, are created by junctures of various block combinations that cause two threads to lie side by side. For example, shaft 4 can be used with either shaft 1 or 2. One of these sheds will place the last thread of a block on shaft 4 in a side-by-side position with the first thread of the block on shaft 1 or 2. When these threads are visible on the surface, they create a slightly open space on the back of the weaving and vice versa. The lines and spaces can appear together on the same face of the weaving. You will encounter these faulty lines as you weave the projects in this chapter although they may not be apparent to you initially because you may be more interested in the interaction of the color and blocks on the surface.

      Tie-ups require only four treadles because only two pattern blocks can be combined with two background blocks, but there are four distinct block combinations. Refer to the Weaving chapter for information on headings, beating, and changing blocks; directions specific to an individual project or to emphasize a certain point are noted with each project.

4-Block, 4-Shaft Projects

Red Rock Runner and Placemats

It was the rugged canyons of "red rock country" near Sedona, Arizona, that inspired this table runner. Layer upon layer of sandstone and shale in shades of rust, browns, and gold conjured up a bright and colorful palette.

The new concept that I present in this runner is the blending of a variety of colors that from a distance read as one. The values of the colors in the pattern and background are close so the differences in hue will be the deciding factor. I had to pick colors carefully to make this work. Even though both the pattern and background are made up of several colors, one group must represent pattern, the other background. An outline thread at the edge of each pattern block adds interest and separates pattern from background. The woven design begins with a small diamond motif near the end of the runner that elongates into a steadily increasing chevron before reversing at the center. Because the design works equally well on either side, the runner is reversible.

PROJECT NOTES

Warp Maysville 8/4 cotton carpet warp in two color groupings:

Background: Mix of red brown #7, dark brown #8, walnut brown #74 (644 yd total)

Pattern: Mix of copper #35, dubonnet #71, dusty rose #19, bronze #40, coral #32 (434 yd total)

Outline: forest green #12 (14 yd), navy blue #5 (14 yd), black #2 (7 yd), purple #25 (7 yd)

Constant: copper #35 (112 yd), navy blue #5 (28 yd), dubonnet #71 (28 yd), forest green #12 (14 yd)

Thick Weft Two 1" strips of fabric the front of one strip wound to the back of the other strip on a rag shuttle

Thin Weft Maysville 8/4 cotton carpet warp in a color to match the fabric

Warp Sett 30 ends per inch, 1 thread per heddle

Reed 15 dent, sleyed 2 ends per dent

Width in Reed 12$^{2}/_{5}$"

Finished Width Same or slightly wider, measured at the fold of the fabric

Total Ends 372

Cloth Length 72"

Raw Length Woven under tension to 87"

Take-up 17% (during weaving) 12$^{1}/_{4}$"

Shrinkage 17% (after weaving) 12$^{1}/_{4}$"

Tie-On 8" (becomes hem)

Hems 1$^{3}/_{4}$" × 2 = 3$^{1}/_{2}$"

Loom Waste 16" (4" per shaft; becomes hem)

Total Warp Length 124" or 3$^{1}/_{2}$ yards

WARP COLOR ORDER

Follow the warp color order and wind a 3$^{1}/_{2}$-yard warp, four threads at a time—two pattern and two background. Constants form the border stripe before joining the mix of brown background threads. The first pattern block begins with one outline thread and one background thread. Each pattern block has a different color outline thread, and the center block is outlined on both sides with the same color to make it symmetrical. There are five mixed pattern colors and three mixed background colors so splice (see Splicing, page 20) the warp colors as you wind them, choosing colors from the mixture. After winding the warp, follow the directions for Warping the Loom (page 25).

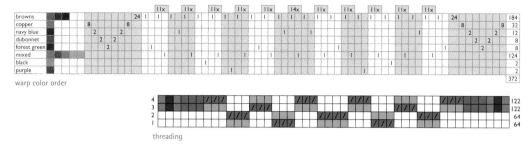

warp color order

threading

THREADING

Thread the mixed colors of both pattern and background randomly. Thread the blocks as usual after threading the constants. The block order reverses in the center.

WEAVING

Spread the warp to the width of the reed by weaving 6–8 picks of 8/4 cotton. Follow the directions for Weaving an Elastic Heading (page 38). After spreading the warp, apply a small amount of flexible fabric glue along the fell line. Do not beat until the glue is totally dry.

Weave a 1³/₄" heading, using the pair of adjacent treadles that will weave the first pattern block.

After weaving the body of the runner, weave 1³/₄" heading with the same pair of treadles that wove the last pattern block. Cut the thin weft and tuck the tail into the same shed. With a contrasting thread of 8/4 cotton, weave 2 picks to mark the cutting line. Apply a small amount of flexible fabric glue along the cutting line. Remove the finished runner from the loom.

FINISHING

Follow the directions for Headings and Hems (page 140).

TIE-UP

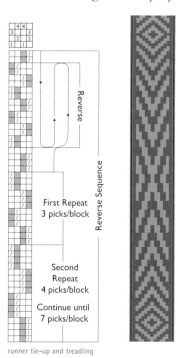

Reverse

Reverse Sequence

First Repeat
3 picks/block

Second
Repeat
4 picks/block

Continue until
7 picks/block

runner tie-up and treadling

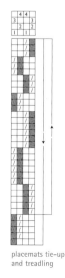

placemats tie-up
and treadling

August Garden Runner and Placemats

As summer waned and the colors of the yarrow, echinacea, sage, lamb's-ear, and dusty miller in my garden dried and mellowed, I adopted their beautiful muted palette for this runner. A soft and subtle print fabric seemed appropriate for the weft.

PROJECT NOTES

Warp Maysville 8/4 cotton carpet warp in mixed colors:

Background: bronze #40 (1008 yd)

Pattern:

Mix 1: sage #33, myrtle green #15, parakeet # 48, aqua #45, kelly green #73 (180 yd total)

Mix 2: limestone gray #36, colonial green #14, aqua green #45, colonial blue #3 (144 yd total)

Mix 3: dubonnet #71, old rose #20, dusty rose #19, rust #67 (144 yd total)

Mix 4: purple #25, navy blue #5, smokey blue #6, dubonnet #71 (27 yd total)

Constants: purple #25 (36 yd), aqua green #45 (36 yd), slate gray #13 (36 yd), old rose #20 (18 yd)

Thick Weft Two 1" strips of fabric, the front of one strip wound to the back of the other strip on a rag shuttle

Thin Weft Maysville 8/4 cotton carpet warp in a color to match the fabric or warp

Warp Sett 30 ends per inch, 1 thread per heddle

Reed 15 dent, sleyed 2 ends per dent

Width in Reed 13⁴/₅"

Finished Width Same or slightly wider, measured at the fold of the fabric

Total Ends 412

Cloth Length 90"

Raw Length Woven under tension to 108¹/₂"

Take-Up 17% (during weaving) 15¹/₃"

Shrinkage 17% (after weaving) 15¹/₃"

Tie-On 16" (becomes fringe)

Loom Waste 16" (4" per shaft; becomes fringe)

Warp Length 153" or 4¹/₄ yards

WARP COLOR ORDER

Follow the warp color order and wind a 4¹/₂-yard warp, two threads at a time—pattern and background. After winding the warp, follow the directions for Warping the Loom (page 25). After warping, tie on and leave 16" hanging free for a twisted fringe.

					20x	16x	16x	56x	16x	16x	20x					
bronze			8		24	1	1	1	1	1	1	1	24			8	224
purple			2			2										2	8
aqua green		2		2										2		2	8
slate gray			2	2										2	2		8
old rose				2											2		4
mix 1						1						1					40
mix 2							1				1						32
mix 3								1		1							32
mix 4									1								56
																412

warp color order

THREADING

4				118
3				118
2				88
1				88

threading

The loom waste will become fringe at the other end of the weaving.

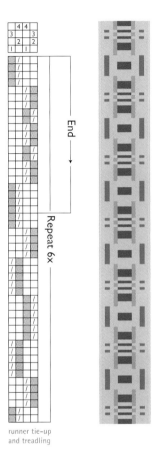

runner tie-up
and treadling

WEAVING

Spread the warp to the width of the reed by weaving 6–8 picks of 8/4 cotton. Follow the directions for Weaving an Elastic Heading (page 38). Continue weaving, following the treadling draft.

FINISHING

Follow the directions for Fringes (page 143).

August Garden Placemats

Weave a set of placemats to accompany the long runner. Use a warp length measurement from another set of placemats based on the number you want to weave. To narrow the placemats to 12³⁄₄" wide, delete a total of 32 ends from the warp. Change the number of threads in Block B to sixteen—eight pattern and eight background. Follow the treadle order for the placemats. The draft contains only 62 picks, but it can be elongated to 68 picks for a better-proportioned mat. Make the necessary adjustments and weave the placemats.

TIE-UP

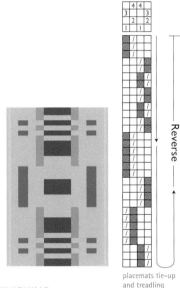

placemats tie-up
and treadling

FINISHING

Make triple-folded hems, following the directions for Headings and Hems (page 140).

Black Canyon of the Gunnison Runner

In this runner, large shifting blocks of strong color interlace with small bright splashes of color to recall glimpses of spring wildflowers against the dark crevices of mighty mountain masses. Constants are used to enlarge adjacent blocks and create bold spaces on which to sprinkle bits of the warm and cool colors reminiscent of wildflowers. Outline threads add a dash of color against the large blocks.

I use the traditional Swedish method of threading two threads per heddle, four per dent, to create a strong, linear feeling in the runner. The weft is a solid

black fabric, almost obscured by the density of the warp. Using a printed calico would be fruitless as its subtle patterns wouldn't be visible. Any printed fabric that showed at the edges might even detract from the strong, bold design.

PROJECT NOTES

Warp Maysville 8/4 cotton carpet warp: black #2 (1140 yd), forest green #12 (372 yd), dubonnet #71 (186 yd), navy blue #5 (372 yd), smokey blue #6 (186 yd), gold #10 (120 yd), burnt orange #18 (120 yd), cranberry #38 (60 yd), Kentucky cardinal #23 (60 yd)

Outline purple #25 (72 yd)

Thick Weft: Two 1" strips of black fabric, the front of one strip wound to the back of the other strip on a rag shuttle

Thin Weft: Maysville 8/4 cotton carpet warp: black #2 to match the fabric

Reed 10 dent, sleyed 4 ends per dent

Warp Sett 40 ends per inch, 2 threads per heddle

Width in Reed 22²/₅"

Finished Width Same or slightly wider, measured at the fold of the fabric

Total Ends 896

Cloth Length 60"

Raw Length Woven under tension to 72"

Take-Up 17% (during weaving) 10¹/₅"

Shrinkage 17% (after weaving) 10¹/₅"

Tie-On 12" (becomes fringe)

Loom Waste 16" (4" per shaft; becomes fringe)

Total Length of Warp 108" or 3 yards

WARP COLOR ORDER

Follow the warp color order and wind a 3-yard warp, holding two pattern and two background threads as you wind. Cut and splice (see Splicing, page 20) where the color changes are indicated. Keep in mind that the pairs of outline threads are the first and last pair of threads of the large blocks. After winding the warp, follow the directions for Warping the Loom (page 25).

THREADING

Thread the constants on shafts 3 and 4 along with the B and D blocks. Thread two threads of the same color in the heddle.

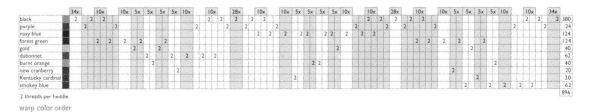

warp color order

threading

TIE-UP

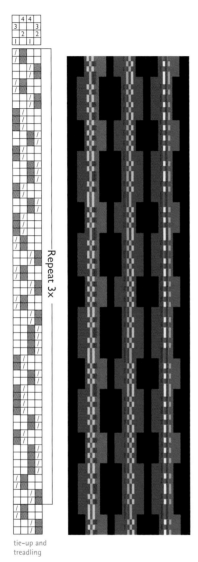

tie-up and
treadling

TIE-ON

Tie this dense warp in small groups to the front tie-rod. Leave 12" hanging free to become twisted fringe at one end. The loom waste will become fringe on the other end.

WEAVING

Spread the warp to the width of the reed by weaving 6–8 picks of 8/4 cotton. Follow the directions for Weaving an Elastic Heading (page 38). When the body of the runner is complete, weave the final heading, using the same pair of treadles that wove the last block.

FINISHING

A bold fringe is a fitting finish for this bold runner. Follow the directions for Fringes (page 143).

Blue Saltillo Runner and Placemats

A visit to an old Spanish Colonial church in Las Trampas, New Mexico, was the inspiration for this long table runner and placemats. Legend has it that when the Las Trampas church, originally known as the Church of the Twelve Apostles, was built, only twelve men at a time were allowed to erect its 4-foot-thick adobe walls. The church, which stands 34 feet tall, was built with an outside choir loft so that the choir could move outside to sing during religious processions.

The stark interior decorated in blue and white, gleaming silver candlesticks adorning the altar, and wooden floors polished from years of use projected a cool, quiet, and serene atmosphere. Outside, an irrigation ditch bringing water to thirsty crops ran along the road leading to this quiet village. These two visions eventually fused in the design of this runner and placemats.

PROJECT NOTES

Warp Maysville 8/4 cotton carpet warp
Background: linen #46 (544 yd)
Pattern: Mix of blues: smokey blue #6, royal blue #4, Spanish blue #72, Oriental royal blue #76 (680 yd total)
Constant: copper #35 (34 yd), red brown #7 (34 yd), bronze #40 (34 yd), burnt orange #18 (17 yd)

Thick Weft Two 1" strips of fabric, the front of one strip wound to the back of the other strip on a rag shuttle

Thin Weft Maysville 8/4 cotton carpet warp in a color to match the fabric or warp

Reed 12 dent, sleyed 2 ends per dent

Warp Sett 24 ends per inch, 1 thread per heddle

Width In Reed 13$\frac{1}{5}$"

Finished Width Same or slightly wider, measured at fold of fabric

Total Ends 316

Cloth Length 90"

Raw Length Woven under tension to 108"

Take-Up (during weaving) 15$\frac{1}{3}$"

Shrinkage (after weaving) 15$\frac{1}{3}$"

Tie-On 16" (becomes fringe)

Loom Waste 16" (4" per shaft; becomes fringe)

Total Warp length 153" or 4$\frac{1}{4}$ yards

WARP COLOR ORDER

Follow the warp color order and wind a 4$\frac{1}{4}$-yard warp, holding one background and one pattern thread as you wind. Cut and splice (see Splicing, page 20) the pattern threads at random. After winding the warp, follow the directions for Warping the Loom (page 25).

THREADING ORDER

The constants, threaded on shafts 3 and 4, form the border.

blues		8				8	4	6	4	4	4	4	8	4	8	24	8	4	8	4	6	4	4	4	6	4	8							8	160
linen						4	6	4	4	4	4	4	8	4	8	24	8	4	8	4	6	4	4	4	6	4									128
copper			2		2																						2			2					8
red brown				2		2																						2		2					8
bronze				2	2																								2	2					8
orange					2																								2						4
																																			316

Thread pattern then ground throughout the blocks.

warp color order

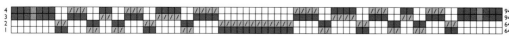

4 94
3 94
2 64
1 64

threading

TIE-UP

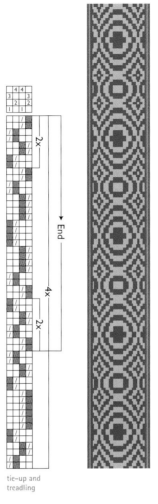

tie-up and treadling

TIE-ON

Tie on, leaving about 16" of warp hanging free to become fringe. The loom waste will become fringe at the other end.

WEAVING

Spread the warp to the width of the reed by weaving 4–6 picks of 8/4 cotton and follow the directions for Weaving an Elastic Heading (page 38). At the end of the body of the runner, continue to weave a 1" heading with the same pair of treadles used to weave the heading at the other end. Loosen the tension and cut at the back tie-rod.

FINISHING

Making the fringe follow the contour of the motif adds to the overall beauty of the runner (you can tie it straight across if you prefer). Look at the motif closest to the end of the runner. From the center Block A of the motif closest to the end of the runner, count to the right and upward eight blocks. The block order is ABCDABCD. At the eighth block—D—the blocks reverse to the selvedge, CBA. This is the contour to follow when making the fringe. Retain 4 picks of the heading as a base for the fringe. Select four strands, two of each color, and twist them together (see Fringes, page 143). Small groups of threads are time-consuming to twist, but the finished fringe is more graceful than if you use more threads in a group.

BLUE SALTILLO PLACEMATS

Weave a set of placemats to accompany the runner. Use a warp length measurement from another set of placemats based on the number you want to weave.

WARP COLOR ORDER

As per Runner.

THREADING

As per Runner.

WEAVING

Spread the warp to the width of the reed by weaving 6–8 picks of 8/4 cotton. Follow the directions for Weaving an Elastic Heading (page 38). Continue weaving, following the treadling draft.

FINISHING

Make triple-folded hems, following the directions for Headings and Hems (page 140).

TIE-UP

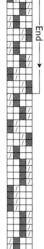

tie-up and treadling

4-Block, 8-Shaft Project

Threading a 4-block design on twice the number of shafts enables you to thread each ABCD block on its own pair of adjacent shafts. In this way, each block may be woven individually or combined with any other block, any two blocks, or all remaining blocks.

Refer to the Weaving chapter for information on headings, beating, and changing blocks. The next project weaves a placemat and uses the blocks individually. Although four blocks must be combined in every shed, one block is a pattern block and the other three are background blocks. There are four combinations.

PRIMROSE PLACEMATS

Here in Arizona, we plant in our gardens the Mexican evening primrose *Oenothera speciosa* "Siskiyou" a low, fast-spreading plant with a delicate, soft pink flower and reddish stamens. Each plant is loaded with new pink blossoms every day throughout the summer. They were the inspiration for this set of placemats for use on the patio.

The placemat design clearly indicates the locations of a plate and flatware. The treadling draft contains variations so that you can weave a different pattern at the ends of each mat. You may also wish to devise your own color scheme to match your (or someone else's) dinnerware.

PROJECT NOTES

Warp Maysville 8/4 cotton carpet warp

Background: linen #46 (697 yd total)

Pattern: Mix of dubonnet #71, copper #35, burnt orange #18, dusty rose #19 (629 yd total)

Thick Weft Two 1" strips of fabric that blends with the warp colors, the front of one strip wound to the back of the other strip on a rag shuttle

Thin Weft Maysville 8/4 cotton carpet warp in a color to match the fabric or warp

Warp Sett 24 ends per inch, 1 thread per heddle

Reed 12 dent, sleyed 2 ends per dent

Width in Reed 12³/₄"

Finished Width Same or slightly wider, measured at the fold of the fabric

Total Ends 304

Number of Placemats Four

Cloth Length Each placemat finished to 18¹/₄" = 74"

Raw Length Each placemat woven under tension to 22"

Take-Up 17% (during weaving) 12³/₅"

Shrinkage 17% (after weaving) 12³/₅"

Tie-On 8"

Hem 8 ends × 1³/₄" = 14"

Loom Waste 32" (4" per shaft)

Warp Length 153" or 4¹/₄ yards

WARP COLOR ORDER

Follow the warp color order and wind a 4¹/₄-yard warp, four threads at a time—two linen background and two pattern ends. The colors are randomly wound in the warp order and randomly threaded in the pattern. Randomly cut off one or both pattern threads and splice in new colors (see Splicing, page 20). Notice the constant stripe of linen along the selvedge. After winding the warp, follow the directions for Warping the Loom (page 25).

THREADING

Each square in the draft represents 8 ends— 4 pattern, 4 background.

TIE-UP

Substitute a different motif for motif 1 in the treadling draft when you want to alter the ends of the mats. Treadle the rest of the mat according to the draft. The tie-up used to weave this project differs from the tie-up order used for 8-shaft patterns thus far for several reasons. Here, each block is used individually. Look at the tie-up and treadling draft. In the previous drafts, only the constants are threaded on shafts 7 and 8 (there is no D block). In the Primrose design, however, the presence of a D block necessitates the change in ties on treadles 3 and 4, 5 and 6. Also, two more

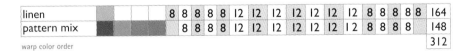

linen				8	8	8	8	8	12	12	12	12	12	12	12	8	8	8	8 8	164
pattern mix					8	8	8	8	12	12	12	12	12	12	12	8	8	8	8	148
																				312

warp color order

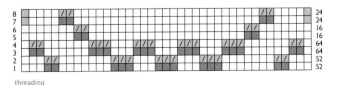

threading

treadles, 9 and 10, are necessary to weave a D block by itself.

WEAVING

Spread the warp to the width of the reed by weaving 6–8 picks of 8/4 cotton. Following the directions for Weaving an Elastic Heading (page 38), weave a 1³⁄₄" heading with the same pair of treadles used to weave the first thick pick. After weaving the body of the mat, weave the second heading with the same pair of treadles that wove the last block.

FINISHING

Make triple-folded hems, following the directions for Headings and Hems (page 140).

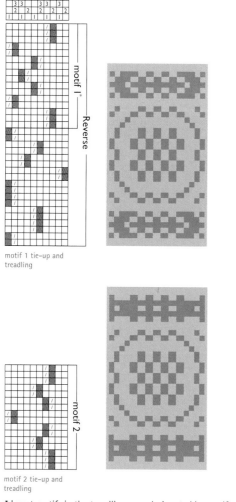

motif 1 tie-up and treadling

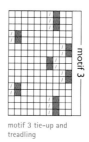

motif 3 tie-up and treadling

motif 2 tie-up and treadling

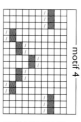

motif 4 tie-up and treadling

* Insert motifs in the treadling area designated by motif 1 for each of the placemats

6-Block Designs

hen designing with six blocks on eight shafts, the ABC blocks are threaded on six shafts, and the last two shafts are kept for the constants. Each block has its own pair of adjacent shafts beginning with the A block on shaft 1. Threading for the DEF blocks begins with the D block on shaft 6 and continues in the opposite order on the same six shafts.

Refer to the Weaving chapter for information on headings, beating, and changing blocks; directions specific to an individual project or to emphasize a certain point are noted with each project.

6-Block, 8-Shaft Projects

Yomud Runner

I draw my design inspiration from my environment. Sometimes there's an obvious, direct correlation, but other times I don't recognize the source of inspiration until later—as happened with the color palette for the Yomud runner. Only after the piece was woven, pressed, and fringed did I realize that the colors were the same as those of a large tribal rug in our dining room, a gift from our son who lives in Kazakhstan, Central Asia.

PROJECT NOTES

Warp Maysville 8/4 cotton carpet warp in the following colors:

Background: burnt orange #18 (90 yd), pink #81 (144 yd), dusty rose #19 (144 yd), Kentucky cardinal #23 (216 yd), velvet #84 (252 yd), navy blue #5 (108 yd)

Pattern: brown #70 (252 yd), walnut brown #74 (90 yd), red brown #7 (144 yd), dark brown #8 (144 yd), copper #35 (252 yd), rust #67 (108 yd)

Thick Weft Two 1" strips of fabric, the front of one strip wound to the back of the other strip on a rag shuttle

Thin Weft Maysville 8/4 cotton carpet warp in a color to match the fabric or warp

Warp Sett 24 ends per inch, 1 thread per heddle

Reed 12 dent, 2 ends per dent

Width in Reed 18"

Finished Width Same or slightly wider measured at fold of the fabric

Total Ends 432

Cloth Length $86^1/_2$"

Raw Length Woven under tension to 104"

Take-Up 17% $14^3/_4$"

Shrinkage 17% $14^3/_4$"

Tie-On 14" (becomes fringe)

Loom Waste 32" (4" per shaft; becomes fringe)

Warp Length 162" or $4^1/_2$ yards

WARP COLOR ORDER

Follow the warp color order and wind a $4^1/_2$-yard warp, holding one pattern and one background thread together for each block. The runner has a narrow constant of 12 ends at each selvedge and each block contains two colors—the first color of each block is pattern; the second color, background. After winding the warp, follow the directions for Warping the Loom (page 25).

THREADING

Because the pattern and background colors are close in value, double-check the color order of the blocks as you thread the heddles.

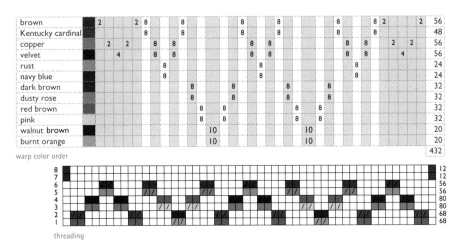

warp color order

threading

TIE-UP

tie-up and treadling

* Designates pick-up rows

TIE-ON

Tie on to the front tie-rod, leaving 16" of warp hanging free to become twisted fringe; the loom waste becomes fringe on the opposite end.

WEAVING

Spread the warp to the width in the reed by weaving 6 to 8 picks of 8/4 cotton weft. Follow the directions for Weaving an Elastic Heading (page 38). Weave a 1" heading, using the same pair of adjacent treadles that will weave the first thick weft. Some of the heading will be removed during finishing. Picking up background threads in the body of the weaving on a pick-up stick (see page 77) allows a slight change in color on the surface. Pick-up points are indicated on the treadling draft by * and yellow blocks. After weaving the body of the runner, weave a 1" heading, using the same pair of treadles used at the beginning. Loosen the tension and cut the warp along the back tie-rod.

FINISHING

This runner is finished with an eight-strand twisted and plied fringe as described in Finishing Techniques (page 139). Small seed knots are tied with two strands each of pattern and background threads. Similar colors are then separated into two groups and twisted and plied simultaneously, ending in a half hitch tied with two of the strands. Because the wide gold stripe contains five seed knots and using all 20 strands would make a fringe too large for a cone, the strands were divided to make three slightly smaller fringes. A tin cone is attached.

Hotevilla Runner and Placemats

Hotevilla, a traditional Third Mesa village in northern Arizona, is the home of a Hopi weaver and friend, Roger Nasevaema. It is also the scene of spring and summer ceremonies at which masked impersonators of kachina—deified ancestral spirits—dance in the plaza. As they dance, the long twisted fringes of the white wedding sashes and colorful handwoven ceremonial sashes sway to and fro with the rhythm of the song. The colors woven into the ceremonial sashes might represent rain, water, clouds, and sky. Memorable and vivid images inspired and contributed to the design and weave of this table runner.

In this 6-block design, the backgrounds of the medium-size blocks are the same color as the pattern of the A and B blocks. Distinguishing pattern and background becomes more difficult because the colors are similar in value. The forest green begins as a constant along the outside edge and then becomes background when combined with the pattern color copper. The first single turquoise outline thread is the first thread of the copper pattern block. The second turquoise outline thread edges the next narrow constant, also copper. The use of outline threads along the edges of the large blocks and constants defines the prominent design elements and separates them from the adjacent central background and small inner pattern blocks.

To weave a Hotevilla Runner and set of placemats from a single warp, refer to the Kayenta Runner and Placemats (page 94) for information on calculating the additional warp length. Weave the runner first at a sett of 30 ends per inch. After cutting off the completed runner, resley the reed to 24 ends per inch and weave the placemats 13" wide.

PROJECT NOTES

Warp: Maysville 8/4 cotton carpet warp in the following colors:
Background: forest green #12 (348 yd)
Blue Range: dark navy blue #82, navy blue #5, smokey blue #6, moody blue #83 (24 yd total)
Red Range: coral #32, copper #35, Kentucky cardinal #23, burnt orange #18 (24 yd total)

Brown Range: rust #67, red brown #7, dark brown #8, copper #35 (24 yd total)
Light Blue Range: duck #47, colonial blue #3, aqua green #45, jade #37 (24 yd total)
Pattern: copper #35 (210 yd), Kentucky cardinal #23 (210 yd)
Center pattern: velvet #84 (15 yd), duck #47 (15 yd), navy blue #5 (15 yd), rust #67 (15 yd)
Outline: turquoise #34 (12 yd), burnt orange #18 (12 yd)

Thick Weft Two 1" strips of fabric, the front of one strip wound to the back of the other on a rag shuttle

Thin Weft 8/4 cotton carpet warp in a color to match the fabric

Warp Sett 30 ends per inch, 1 thread per heddle

Reed 15 dent, sleyed 2 ends per dent

Width in Reed 10½"

Finished Width Same or slightly wider, measured at fold of fabric

Total Ends 316

Cloth Length 40"

Raw Length Woven under tension to 48"

Take-Up 17% (during weaving) 6⅘"

Shrinkage 17% (after weaving) 6⅘"

Tie-On 20" (becomes fringe)

Loom Waste 32" (4" per shaft; becomes fringe)

Total Warp Length 106" or 3 yards

WARP COLOR ORDER

Follow the warp color order and wind a 3-yard warp, two threads at a time—one pattern, one background.

Cut off and splice (see Splicing, page 20) when mixing the color order. After winding the warp, follow the directions for Warping the Loom (page 25).

THREADING

When threading the shafts, the threads will be in pairs from the lease sticks in the order they were wound; you may need to switch some of them at the block changes. As you thread, check the warp order and compare it to the threading order.

TIE-ON

Tie on to the front tie-rod, leaving 15" of warp hanging free to become knots and twisted fringe. The loom waste will become knots and twisted fringe at the other end. (If you're weaving the placemats on the same warp, leave space between the runner and the first placemat for the runner's second fringe and the first placemats first hem.)

TIE-UP

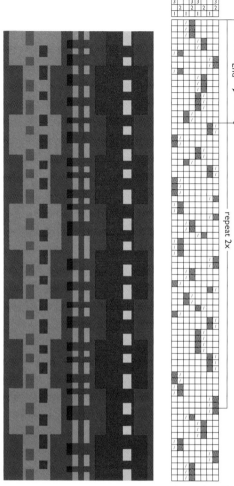

tie-up and treadling

• alternate thread color for placemats.

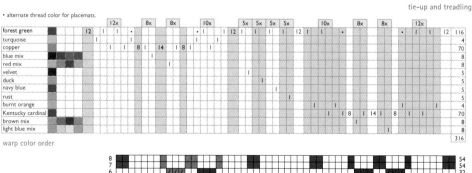

warp color order

threading

WEAVING

Spread the warp to the width in the reed by weaving 6–8 picks of 8/4 cotton. Following the directions for Weaving an Elastic Heading (page 38), weave a 1" heading. Follow the treadling draft to weave the runner, weaving the thick weft first, followed by the thin. Omit the thin pick (tie-down) only when the tie-down shed happens to be the next pattern (thick-pick) shed. Weave the last heading with the same pair of treadles used to weave the last thick pick. If you are not weaving the placemats, loosen the warp tension and cut along the back tie-rod.

FINISHING

The runner is finished with four-strand seed knots, each of whose strands are divided into two groups and twisted into a four-strand fringe. The ends of the fringe are tied with a single strand to keep them small so that a copper cone can be threaded onto the fringe. Follow the directions for Knots (page 141), Fringes (page 143), and Cones or Beads (pages 147).

Hotevilla Placemats

WEAVING

Spread the warp to the width in the reed by weaving 6–8 picks of 8/4 cotton. Follow the directions for Weaving an Elastic Heading (page 38). Continue weaving, following the treadling draft.

FINISHING

Make triple-folded hems, following the directions for Headings and Hems (page 140).

TIE-UP

tie-up and treadling

8-Block Designs

esign possibilities increase with each addition of blocks and shafts. An 8-block pattern threaded on eight shafts gives the maximum design possibilities on an 8-shaft loom. Threading eight blocks on eight shafts requires that each of the ABCD blocks be threaded on a separate adjacent pair of shafts; the order is then reversed to thread the EFGH blocks. Every shed automatically produces four pattern and four background blocks, and there are sixteen possible block combinations. If the design contains a constant, it shares a pair of shafts with another block. It is not likely that all these combinations would be used in a single weaving; however, a universal tie-up makes all the combinations possible on ten treadles by pressing two treadles at a time for each shed. If all sixteen combinations are not required, treadles are tied up in the usual manner.

Refer to the Weaving chapter for information on headings, beating, and changing blocks; directions specific to an individual project or to emphasize a certain point are noted with each project.

8-Block, 8-Shaft Project

Isabelle Placemats

My mother, Sarah Isabelle Ball, "Belle" for short, participated in one of my workshops. Students moved from loom to loom in round-robin fashion, weaving samples of each project. Changes in tie-ups were occasionally made to demonstrate the differences in pattern and design.

When Belle moved to the 8-block pattern on an 8-shaft loom, she was not feeling very confident after the tie-up was altered, as there was no treadling draft to follow. Instructed to design her own weaving and apply what she'd learned from weaving previous samples, she experimented and wove this design. During the critique at the end of the workshop, I asked who had woven such an interesting design with crosses in the center and at four points along the outside edges. Belle shyly admitted that the sample was hers. Workshop participants were thrilled with her resulting design, and so was I. I tell this story to emphasize that sometimes in our weaving, the old adage that "ignorance is bliss" is truly a wonderful virtue.

For these placemats, I have kept Belle's original design intact but added borders at the ends to suggest the placement of flatware and to increase the length of the mat (the central motif clearly indicates the placement of a plate.) Even without a place setting upon it, a placemat's design elements should indicate its purpose.

This 8-block, 8-shaft placemat contains twenty-three pattern colors. Select and arrange colors on a table so that they progress smoothly from one color range to the next before the warp is wound. If you substitute your own colors, do the same, making a list of the colors and their color numbers.

PROJECT NOTES

Warp Maysville 8/4 cotton carpet warp in the following colors:
Background: linen #46 (1356 yd)

Pattern: forest green #12, dark navy blue #82, navy blue #5, royal blue #4, smokey blue #6, purple #25, dubonnet #71, cranberry #38, Kentucky cardinal #23, red #22, poppy red #41, burnt orange #18, coral #32, dusty rose #19, old rose #20, peach #11, copper #35, rust #67, brown #70, red brown #7, walnut brown #74, dark brown #8, velvet #84 (1356 yd total)

Thick Weft Two 1" strips of fabric, the front of one strip wound to the back of the other strip on a rag shuttle

Thin Weft Maysville 8/4 cotton carpet warp in a color to match the fabric or warp

Warp Sett 30 ends per inch, 1 thread per heddle

Reed 15 dent, sleyed 2 ends per dent

Width in Reed 11³/₄"

Finished Width Same or slightly wider, measured at the fold of the fabric

Total Ends 352

Number of Placemats Eight

Cloth Length Each placemat finished to 19¹/₂" = 156" total

Raw Length Each placemat woven under tension to 23¹/₂"

Take Up 17% (during weaving) 26¹/₂"

Shrinkage 17% (after weaving) 26¹/₂"

Tie-On 8"

Hems 1³/₄" × 16 ends = 28"

Loom Waste 32" (4" per shaft)

Total Warp Length 277" or 7³/₄ yards

WARP COLOR ORDER

Follow the warp color order and wind a 7 3/4-yard warp. Load the spool rack from left to right beginning with the first four pattern colors within a color range, for example, four tubes in the blue range. Below them, place four tubes of the background color. This arrangement facilitates changing and rearranging the pattern colors and avoids tangles. For ease during winding and threading, wind with four pattern colors and four background threads at a time. Tie all eight ends together and keep a pattern and a background thread together as a pair and place a finger between each set of adjoining pairs as you wind the warp. All eight threads move through the cross together, and each completed pass through the cross yields 16 ends—8 pattern, 8 background. When it's time to change a color, stop, secure the threads by winding them around the peg on the board or mill, temporarily hold the group with a spring clamp, and cut off the leftmost pattern thread and remove the tube. Shift the remaining three tubes one position to the left so that the tube that was second is now first and add a new color at the right. Rearranging the tubes on the spool rack every bout takes time; proceed slowly and carefully.

Wind the warp in two halves, the first half equaling 176 threads (88 pattern, 88 background). Tie the cross and cinch ties and remove the warp from the board or mill. Begin the second half of the warp where you left off but shift the colors to the left and add the next new color on the right. Four pattern and four background colors are used consistently until near the end of winding the warp. The second half of the warp is slightly different than the first half in order to complete the warp with the exact number of threads. Add the ninth new color and wind as before—this half of the warp now contains nine bouts of 16 ends, or 144 threads. Cut off and discard the pattern as well as the background thread on the left side of the spool rack; this is the first time that both threads are cut off. Wind two bouts with the remaining 3 pattern and 3 background threads, an additional 24 threads. Next, cut off as before, and wind 2 pattern, 2 background threads once, for 8 additional threads. The thread count is now 176 for the second half of the warp. Tie the cross and cinch ties, remove from the board or mill. Lay the two halves of the warp in the correct color order and insert the lease sticks. Follow the directions for Warping the Loom (page 25).

THREADING

There are eight blocks in this design, and threading the ABCD blocks uses all eight shafts; the EFGH blocks must be threaded in the opposite order. Because two different blocks share the same pair of shafts, the block combinations within a design are somewhat

background	14	9	14	9	14	9	14	9	14	9	14	9	14	9	14	175
color wash	14	9	14	9	14	9	14	9	14	9	14	9	14	9	14	175
warp color order																350

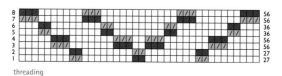

threading

limited. For example, it is impossible to have the pattern of Block A and pattern of Block E visible at the same time. Every shed is made up of four pattern and four background blocks. Follow the draft and begin threading the HGFE blocks; the ABCD blocks are threaded in the center of the design. The arrangement and placement of colors when threading are up to you. To avoid having two pattern or two background threads lie next to each other between the E and D blocks, reverse the order of entering the threads in the heddle: if you were threading pattern-background in Block E, begin Block D by threading background-pattern, or vice versa. This places the adjoining pattern or background threads in opposite sheds.

TIE-UP

Treadle 1 weaves Block A; treadle 3, Blocks AB; treadle 5, Blocks AC; and treadle 7, Blocks ABCD. The treadles are tied to

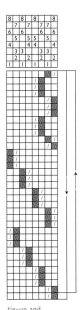
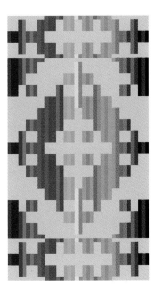

tie-up and treadling

progress from left to right, weaving a large chevron by increasing the pattern blocks from the center out in order from Block A to Blocks ABCD. The block order continues by treadling 2, 4, 6, and 8, increasing the pattern blocks one at a time to EFGH. Note that the design reverses from pattern to background, or positive to negative, in the center. When the treadling order is reversed, a large diamond shape results.

WEAVING

Spread the warp to the width of the reed by weaving 6–8 picks of 8/4 cotton. Follow the directions for Weaving an Elastic Heading (page 38) and weave a $1^3/_4$" heading, using the same pair of adjacent treadles that weave the first block. End the last pick of thin weft on treadle 8 and leave the shuttle attached. Step on treadle 7 and begin weaving the thick weft from the same side that the thin weft exited. Taper the end, wrap the selvedge, and tuck the tail into the same shed. Continue weaving with alternating thin and thick wefts. After the eleventh thick pick, thrown on treadle 7, notice that the tie-down shed happens to be the next four block combination and that the sheds are opposite each other. Here, omit the thin pick and throw the thick pick in its place. Do the same again at the corresponding point at the other end of the placemat. To end the mat, weave a $1^3/_4$" elastic heading and then weave 2 picks of a brightly colored thread to mark the cutting line. Weave a $1^3/_4$" heading for the next mat.

FINISHING

Make triple-folded hems, following the directions for Headings and Hems (page 140).

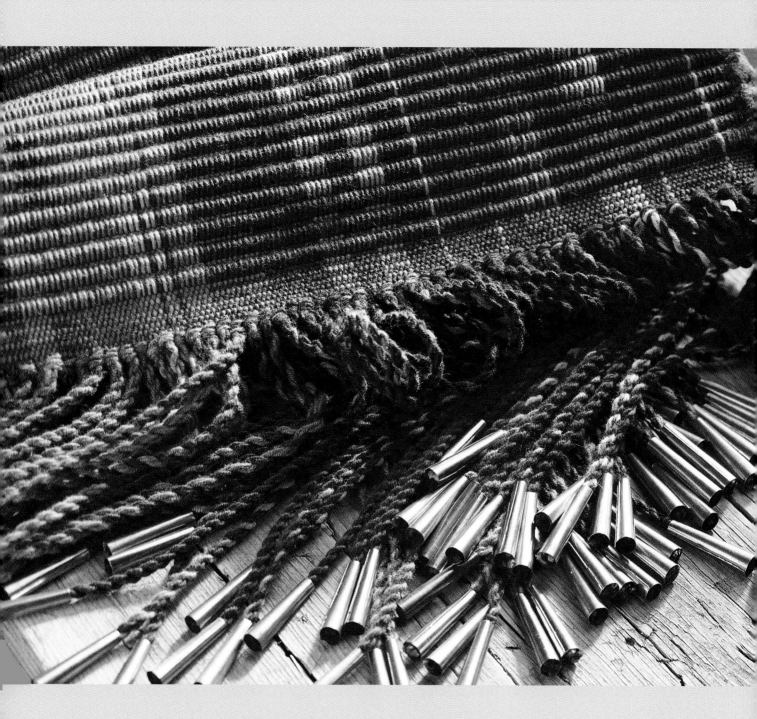

Finishing and Care

inishing is as important as weaving; large and small finishing details can make or break the overall weaving. You'll want to consider how the warp ends will be treated—will they be hemmed, knotted, or fringed? Will the finished weaving be washed, by hand or machine, or dry-cleaned? Whatever decisions you make about finishing, they should always aim to enhance and embellish the weaving.

You'll also want to consider embellishments—knots, fringes, cones, and beads. Embellishments add interest and beauty to table runners, rugs, and hangings. Think about how the heading will be held in place—will knots be tied first, then twisted into fringe, or will the fringe be twisted without a knot? If the warp sett is very close, there may not be room for the knots to lie neatly side by side. In that case, how will the twisted fringe begin and end? Would you like to make a fringe thicker or more substantial? Perhaps you would like to add a cone or bead at the end of the fringe. Density of the warp plays a large part in finding the right solution. You must answer all of these questions before you can begin finishing.

Headings and Hems

Headings and hems are addressed together as every piece woven in rep requires a heading, and an elongated heading has the potential to become a hem. In addition, a single hemming technique is used on everything from tableware to rugs and wall hangings. Not only does a heading help maintain compression in the weave and keep the weave from backing out, it also defines the beginning and end of the weave. Knowing how to weave a heading correctly (see page 38) can save time and frustration, as once the heading is woven incorrectly, there is no going back. Everyone has seen an otherwise beautiful rug that refuses to lie flat on the floor, usually because the heading is woven too narrow for the width of the woven rug, causing the end to draw up and flip over.

Here's how to get the heading to match the width of the rug:

1. Place the woven piece face down on a table with the working edge facing you and place a heavy object on top to stabilize it. Working section by section, remove the excess heading in 1"–2" increments and, if the project has a knotted or twisted fringe, tie the knots or twist the fringe before removing the next increment. If all the excess is removed at the same time, the weaving may begin to back out (see Figure 1, page 141).

2. For a project with a hem, apply a small amount of archival flexible fabric glue close to the edge where you will cut and then turn it under for the hem of the elongated heading. Trim off the excess warp ends to the glued part of the elongated heading. When hemming a series of placemats, make a zigzag with the glue across the two parallel weft picks marking the cutting line between two placemats. Spread the glue with your finger. Allow the glue to dry completely.

3. Cut between the two parallel weft picks to separate the placemats.

4. Fold up one-third of the heading and finger-press in a straight line. Fold again, bringing the first folded edge up to the first thick pick. Finger-press; the heading will stay pressed while you work.

5. Machine-stitch with matching thread, about 10 stitches per inch. Be careful not to stretch the hem when sewing.

Knots

Seed knots—small overhand knots tied against a heading—not only hold the weaving securely but add a decorative touch. When combined with a twisted fringe, the knots add another element of decoration. If you look carefully, you'll see that one side of a seed knot looks better than the other. To make the knot's best side face toward the right side of your piece, turn the weaving over and tie the knots on the back.

1. Place the woven item face down on a table with the working edge facing you and place a heavy object on top to stabilize it. Place the end of the weaving along the edge of the table so that your hands have room to work below. If you need to remove excess heading, cut and remove it by 1"–2" increments to keep the heading from moving until the knots are tied (Figure 1).

2. Because small knots look better than big ones, use between 4 and 8 strands per knot. Select the number of threads for the knot.

The following steps are written for right-handers; if you are left-handed, read "right" for "left" and vice versa.

3. Place your left palm up on the weaving at the edge of the table. Extend the first two fingers and fold up the last two; the thumb sticks upward. With the right hand pull the strands up, over, and around the extended fingers, ending by holding the ends with the left thumb (Figure 2).

4. Slightly spread the first two fingers of the left hand so that you can reach between

FIGURE 1

FIGURE 2

FIGURE 3

FIGURE 4

FIGURE 5

them and grasp the loose ends; pull out to the right and down (Figure 3 and 4).

5. With the palm still up, fold up the first two fingers and pivot the left hand so that the loop spans the fingers. Pull the end of the strand toward yourself while exerting slight pressure with the bent fingers. The knot will shift to the left (Figure 5).

6. Slightly rotate the fingers in the loop, pulling on the left side to position the half-knot as close to the heading as possible (Figure 6).

FIGURE 6

7. With tension on the strands in your right hand, move the index finger and thumb to just below the half-knot. Pinch and hold (Figure 7).

8. Remove the left fingers from the loop and pull the loose ends toward you.

You have just made a seed knot as close to the heading as possible. With practice, it will become easier. After you have made a few knots, turn the weaving over and look at the knots on the right side of the weaving. Compare the front and back of the knots. Do you agree that they look better when tied from the back?

FIGURE 7

In the following projects, I tied seed knots before adding the fringe. The Hotevilla Runner (page 128) is tied with four-strand seed knots, each of whose strands are divided into two groups and twisted into a four-strand fringe. The ends of the fringe are tied with a single strand to keep them small so that a copper cone can be threaded onto the fringe. The Yomud Runner (page 124) is also tied with four-strand seed knots. Two seed knots are combined to make an eight-strand twisted fringe except in the wide gold stripe. Because the stripe contains five seed knots and using all 20 strands would make a fringe too large for a cone, the strands were divided to make three slightly smaller fringes. If you plan to add a cone or bead to a fringe, make sure before you begin that your fringe will fit into the hole. See page 147 for adding cones or beads.

Fringes

Fringe added to a weaving can be twisted whether or not a seed knot is tied, but five to eight rows of heading need to remain intact. A traditional Swedish twisted fringe consists of two groups of multiple strands of threads that are spun and plied simultaneously. The result is an accurately controlled and precisely measured fringe. The number of warp ends per group depends on the size and thickness of the fringe. As few as two threads make a fine delicate fringe; tableware looks best on a placement with a four- to six-strand twisted fringe. More strands per group make heavier, aesthetically pleasing finishes suitable for rugs. Before embarking on a big project, try to visualize the result and make a few test knots and fringes before.

For example, in the rug titled "1910 Revisited" on page 70, eight pairs of warp ends were used to make the twisted fringe. The fringe is tied up against a heading that contains seven weft picks, enough to make a clear demarcation between the rug and the fringe. Here's how that fringe was made:

1. Place the woven piece facedown on a table with the working edge facing you and place a heavy object on top to stabilize it. Allowing five to eight rows of heading to remain, cut and remove any excess weft in 1"–2" increments just before the fringe is twisted.

2. This twisted fringe is made with sixteen warp ends divided into two groups of four pairs each. Hold each group with your thumb and index finger, one group in each hand, in preparation for twisting (Figure 1).

FIGURE 1

3. Straighten each group and tie a half-knot, the right group over the left (Figure 2).

FIGURE 2

4. Pull the half-knot close to the heading (Figure 3).

FIGURE 3

5. Hold each group under tension and twist to the right once. Do not over twist (Figure 4). The strands will kink up if you over twist them.

FIGURE 4

6. Pass the right group over the left. Continue until you have twisted and passed the strands a total of fourteen times (Figure 5).

FIGURE 5

FIGURE 6

FIGURE 7

7. Measure the length of the first fringe (Figure 6) and compare the length of each subsequent fringe to it (Figure 7).

8. Pinch and hold the twisted fringe with the left index finger and thumb while straightening the strands in the right group. Apply a slight pressure with the right thumbnail and finger to smooth and straighten these threads (Figure 8).

FIGURE 8

9. Take the smoothed threads up and over to the left, and behind the twisted fringe, bringing the ends around far enough to be pulled through the loop (Figure 9).

FIGURE 9

10. Use a crochet hook to lift the ends through the loop (Figure 10).

FIGURE 10

11. Hold the twisted fringe in the left hand and tighten the loop (Figure 11). You have completed a half hitch around the fringe with the right group.

FIGURE 11

12. Continue to hold the twisted fringe in the left hand. Pull slightly with the right hand to tighten the half hitch. Do not pull on the left group as it will slide up and compress (Figure 12).

FIGURE 12

When a heavier or thicker fringe is needed, you can tie in additional strands of warp threads. Cut the extra ends to be added twice as long as the fringe will be and lay them between the two groups of ends to be twisted. Tie the right group over left group and pull up to the heading as in steps 2 and 3. Continue laying in additional strands. The extra warps will not be noticeable. If the fringe does not require additional strands, it is possible to make a twisted fringe without first tying right over left. Instead, begin the twist with step 4 and continue. Try both techniques and use the one you prefer.

Cones or Beads

If you would like to add cones or beads, tie the half hitch at the end of the fringe with only one or two strands. Otherwise, the knot will be too large to fit inside the cone (or bead). Thread a needle large enough to accommodate the four (or more) strands of the fringe and also fit through the cone or bead (Figure 1).

Tie an overhand knot on top of the half-hitch knot and pull the cone down over it. When you have threaded all the cones onto the fringe, adjusted them until they are even. You may have to loosen and retie a few of the knots (Figure 3). The more carefully you work, the less adjustment will be necessary.

FIGURE 1

FIGURE 3

Pass the needle through the small end of the cone and slide the cone or bead up the fringe (Figure 2).

FIGURE 2

CARE

Whether you've woven a utilitarian rep rug or a decorative hanging, you put in the same painstaking, time-consuming effort in planning and executing it. Now that it's finished, you want to preserve and maintain its quality and beauty.

Washing

Washing removes surface dirt and debris, restoring your woven piece to near-new condition. Whether you can wash a rep-woven piece depends on its size and the availability of a tub or other container large enough to accommodate it. Many are too heavy and solid and too resistant to crumpling to fit into a washing machine. Placemats, however, can easily be washed in cool water and mild detergent in a kitchen sink or laundry tub, and large rugs can be washed in a bathtub. Washing is not recommended for pieces embellished with cones as they may rust or discolor.

Fold the rug accordion style into sudsy water and move it up and down to loosen dirt particles and debris. Rinse several times in cool water and stand to drain until manageable. Lay flat on towels, or hang over a railing so the item is evenly and well supported while drying. Turn the rug over periodically to hasten the drying. Small items can be washed in the same manner and should dry flat on towels, turning periodically as well. Don't use an automatic dryer as they tend to shrink and deform the item and the constant tumbling weakens the threads.

Starching

A generous coat of spray starch preserves the crisp look of a rep-woven piece by giving the surface a harder finish as well as adding a protective coating that resists dirt and penetration from spills. After completing hems, knots, and fringes, take your finished weaving outdoors, position it nearly vertically, and saturate both sides with spray starch or sizing. I use Faultless, a professional-formula heavy starch. Roll the weaving in cloth or plastic while wet, and allow it to dry slowly so the starch has time to penetrate. Depending on the humidity level where you live, you don't want to leave it rolled for more than 24 hours or it could mildew. Press when dry. Hold the iron using steam about 1" above the item allowing the fibers to fill with steam, then press lightly. This procedure also swells and relaxes the warp threads, contributing to the shrinkage that occurs off the loom. A light application of starch after each washing helps maintain the appearance of your woven piece.

A rug may be too large to iron. When that's the case, I starch the rug and hang it over a railing protected with a sheet of plastic. Turn the rug several times while drying.

Dry Cleaning

Dry cleaning is gentler on a rep-woven piece than washing and helps keep a crisp look without disturbing the surface of the weaving. The dry cleaner can apply a protective finish to further retard staining and soiling. Dry cleaning is an ideal method for caring for rep-woven clothing, large rugs, and tableware. Although it is expensive, the cost is justified to prolong the life of a beautiful piece of work.

Cones or beads added to a weaving need special care. I sew a muslin bag the width of the weaving and about 4"–5" deep, slip it over fringe embellished with cones or beads at each end of the weaving, and slip-stitch it shut to the heading. The bag keeps the fringe from tangling during dry cleaning.

Beyond Rep Adaptation for Contemporary Application

Clothing

I discovered rep-woven garment-weight fabric by accident. While experimenting with 8/2 cotton warp for towels, I cut ³/₈"-wide strips of fabric printed with a floral pattern and used them as weft. Lightly beaten, the first fabric strip folded neatly into thirds and lay perfectly flat. As I continued adding strips, it became evident that the floral image in the fabric could be reconstructed and, at the same time, the two-color warp of the rep weave was visible on the surface, producing an image like a hologram. It is the alternation of thick and thin wefts that produces the image on the surface. Because the fabric strips were cut with the grain, they folded easily and neatly and produced a lightweight, wrinkle-resistant fabric. It was possible to alternate two, even three or four unrelated fabrics at random and still visually reconnect the original images in the newly woven rep fabric. My excitement at this discovery led me to create hundreds of yards of lightweight yardage that I sewed into vests and jackets.

Unmercerized cotton—8/2, 10/2, 12/2, 16/2, 20/2, 22/2, 30/2—whether used in a single size or in combination, works well as a warp for rep yardage. When pressed with an iron using steam, the warp ends shrink slightly, which pulls the fabric strips slightly closer together. Rep-woven fabric is stable both warpwise and weftwise, making it possible to cut pattern pieces in either direction.

151

Towels

The same 8/2 unmercerized cotton warp used for yardage gives rep-woven towels the absorbency, hand, and softness required of a tea towel. For towels, I use 8/2 cotton as the thick weft and sewing thread for the tie-down weft. A long, narrow spool of Mettler or Gutermann sewing thread fits neatly into a small boat shuttle. Although weaving is slow, seeing the image appear is intriguing, which stimulates productivity.

Cards

Necessity is the mother of invention when it comes to finding a new solution to an old problem. To pay my rent as a member of a cooperative gallery, I found that it was easier to sell a large number of small, inexpensive objects rather than a few larger ones. I first tried mounting small pieces of fabric left over from vests and jackets on card stock and inserting them into clear plastic bags along with a sheet of stationery and an envelope; I called them handwoven gift cards. Sales increased, which encouraged me, but it was clear that I needed to create the cards more swiftly and efficiently. My solution was to weave eight at a time, side by side, each strip woven with different fabrics. Each new warp produces a different image on the surface, and no two cards are alike. To weave the cards, I first weave a heading, then weave the strips of fabric about 5" long and end with a heading. I leave about 1" of unwoven warp and begin the next strip. After taking them off the loom, I stabilize the long strips of woven fabric, fusing them to card stock using a product called HeatNbond, ironing it to the back of the strips of cards, then cut the cards apart before packaging. Several thousand cards later, the method has proven cost effective and profitable. I've learned that it pays to dream of what might be possible; reaching a solution is an exciting and stimulating exercise as well as an artistic challenge.

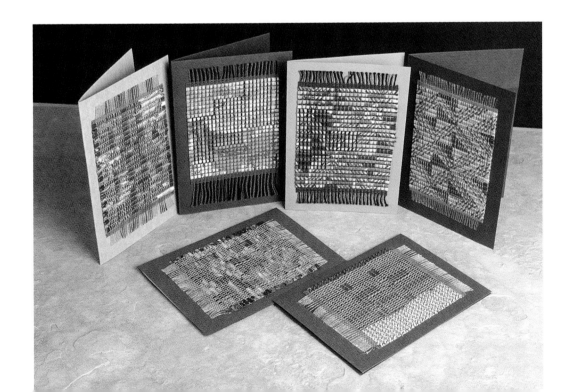

Framed Weaving

Framing is another way to market pieces of woven textiles. I sew selected weavings along the edges to acid-free foam core whose cut edge I've covered with black acid-free masking tape to make it less visible. I sew by pulling a small threaded needle through the textile and foam core at 1" intervals, using needle-nose pliers to pull the needle. The fabric on the foam core is adhered to a larger piece of foam core which is covered in linen. I then have a professional framer mount the completed foam cores into the frame. I don't recommend covering the textile with glass as it creates an undesirable visual and tactile barrier between the textile and the viewer. To remove dust, you can lightly vacuum the textile.

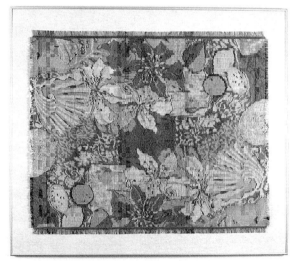

The Great Unknown

When I wove my first piece of rep weave, more than twenty-five years ago, I didn't intend to weave more than a few pieces in that weave. Ha! Happy accidents that I didn't want to abandon led to each and every new development, and experimenting with different sizes and types of fibers has led to further exciting results. Many hundreds of table runners, placemats, and wall weavings came first—I couldn't stop. Then came years of experimenting with what might happen if I tried the unknown. That's where I am today, and I'm not done yet. I hope you, too, will be caught up in a technique you find impossible to give up.

Yarn Resource and Color Guide

Maysville carpet warp is the predominant warp and weft used in this book. It is available through your local weaving shop, mail-order catalogs, and the Internet. If you have trouble locating it, please contact the Edgemont Yarn Service and Oriental Rug Company, PO Box 205, Washington, KY 41096; (606) 759-7614; Edgemont@maysvilleky.net.

Maysville Carpet Warp—A Bit of History

January & Wood Company, the oldest family owned cotton mill in the United States, established the Maysville Cotton Mills in 1824 in Maysville, Kentucky. The original mill was completed in 1831. Maysville carpet warp in black, white, ecru, primary and secondary colors, has been manufactured since 1879, and Maysville rug filler since 1930. The Maysville Weavers Guild was started in 1926 and published newsletters containing projects, pictures, and letters from weavers; at one time it reached 40,000 members. The newsletter continued until 1965. Edgemont Yarn Service was started in 1955, and today Maysville spins and dyes over 40 colors of 8/4 cotton carpet warp. In 1990, Edgemont bought the Oriental Rug Company and continues to spin and dye a range of both the Commercial Color and Boil Proof lines.

Color Guide

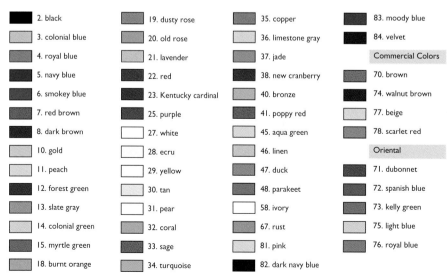

2. black	19. dusty rose	35. copper	83. moody blue
3. colonial blue	20. old rose	36. limestone gray	84. velvet
4. royal blue	21. lavender	37. jade	Commercial Colors
5. navy blue	22. red	38. new cranberry	70. brown
6. smokey blue	23. Kentucky cardinal	40. bronze	74. walnut brown
7. red brown	25. purple	41. poppy red	77. beige
8. dark brown	27. white	45. aqua green	78. scarlet red
10. gold	28. ecru	46. linen	Oriental
11. peach	29. yellow	47. duck	71. dubonnet
12. forest green	30. tan	48. parakeet	72. spanish blue
13. slate gray	31. pear	58. ivory	73. kelly green
14. colonial green	32. coral	67. rust	75. light blue
15. myrtle green	33. sage	81. pink	76. royal blue
18. burnt orange	34. turquoise	82. dark navy blue	

Weaving Record

Date: _____ Project: _____ Pattern Classification: _____

Warp: _____ Weft: _____ Reed: _____

Warp Sett: _____ Width in Reed: _____ Finished Width: _____

Total Ends: _____

Cloth Length: _____ Raw Length: _____ Fringe or Hems: _____

Take-Up & Shrinkage: _____ Tie-On: _____ Loom Waste: _____

Total Length (Convert to Yards): _____

_____ Yards Warp

_____ Yards Weft (about 2/3 Warp)

_____ Total Yardage

Divide total yards by yards per pound or tube, etc.

Profile and Threading:

Important Additional Notes _____

_____

_____

_____

Warp Weight: _____ Date Wound: _____ Date Loom Dressed: _____

Time to Weave Each Piece: _____ Date Finished: _____

Finished Weight of Warp & Weft: Yield: _____ How Many Pieces: _____

Weight of Each Piece: _____

Destination: _____ Price (Retail) Each Piece: _____

Price (Wholesale) Each Piece: _____ Commission %: _____

Cost of Fiber: _____ Source of Fiber: _____ Source of Fabric Weft: _____

Sample or Photo:

Bibliography

Atwater, Mary Meigs. *Byways in Handweaving: An Illustrated Guide to Rare Weaving Techniques.* New York: Macmillan, 1954.

Black, Mary E. *The Key to Weaving.* 2d rev. ed. 1957. Reprint, New York: Macmillan, 1979.

Blomberg, Nancy J. *Navajo Textiles: The William Randolph Hearst Collection.* Tucson: University of Arizona Press, 1988.

Bress, Helene. *The Weaving Book.* New York: Charles Scribner's Sons, 1981.

Carlstedt, Catharina, and Ylva Kongbäck. *Rep.* Helsingborg, Sweden: AB Boktryck, 1987.

Cyrus-Zetterström, Ulla. *Manual of Swedish Handweaving.* 2d U.S. ed. Massachusetts: Charles T. Branford Co., 1977.

Harbert, Nancy. *New Mexico.* Compass American Guides. New York: Random House, 1996.

Haury, Emil W. *The Hohokam Desert Farmers and Craftsmen.* Tucson: University of Arizona Press, 1976.

Johnson, Astrid, Sylvia Mellqvist-Johansson, and Eva Lisa Nordin. *Vackra trasmattor och andra vävar.* Sweden: ICA Bokförlag, 1983.

Lundell, Laila. *Rep Weaves.* Västerås, Sweden: ICA - förlaget AB, 1987.

Nylén, Anna-Maja. *Swedish Handcraft*: New York: Van Nostrand Reinhold, 1977.

Regensteiner, Else. *The Art of Weaving.* New York: Van Nostrand Reinhold, 1970.

Strickler, Carol. *A Weaver's Book of 8-Shaft Patterns from the Friends of Handwoven.* Loveland, Colorado: Interweave Press, 1991.

Wormington, H. M. *Prehistoric Indians of the Southwest.* Denver, Colorado: Denver Museum of Natural History, 1959.

Wright, Barton. *Kachinas: A Hopi Artist's Documentary.* Flagstaff, Arizona: Northland Press with the Heard Museum, 1973.

Zielinski, S. A. *Encyclopaedia of Hand-Weaving.* New York: Funk & Wagnalls, 1959.

Index